PATHWAYS

SECOND EDITION

Listening, Speaking, and Critical Thinking

Teacher's Guide

**NATIONAL
GEOGRAPHIC**
L E A R N I N G

Australia • Brazil • Mexico • Singapore • United Kingdom • United States

NATIONAL
GEOGRAPHIC
L E A R N I N G

Pathways Teacher's Guide 2,
Listening, Speaking, and Critical Thinking,
Second Edition

Publisher: Sherrise Roehr

Executive Editor: Laura Le Dréan

Managing Editor: Jennifer Monaghan

Senior Development Editor: Mary Whittemore

Associate Development Editors: Lisl Bove and
Jennifer Williams-Rapa

Director of Global and U.S. Marketing:
Ian Martin

Product Marketing Manager: Tracy Bailie

Media Research: Leila Hishmeh

Senior Director, Production: Michael Burggren

Manager, Production: Daisy Sosa

Content Project Manager: Mark Rzeszutek

Senior Digital Product Manager: Scott Rule

Manufacturing Planner: Mary Beth
Hennebury

Interior and Cover Design: Brenda Carmichael

Art Director: Brenda Carmichael

Composition: MPS North America LLC

For product information and technology assistance, contact us at
Cengage Learning Customer & Sales Support, cengage.com/contact

For permission to use material from this text or product,
submit all requests online at **cengage.com/permissions**
Further permissions questions can be emailed to
permissionrequest@cengage.com

ISBN: 978-1-337-56247-8

National Geographic Learning
20 Channel Center Street
Boston, MA 02210
USA

National Geographic Learning, a Cengage Learning Company, has a mission
to bring the world to the classroom and the classroom to life. With our English
language programs, students learn about their world by experiencing it. Through
our partnerships with National Geographic and TED Talks, they develop the
language and skills they need to be successful global citizens and leaders.

Locate your local office at **international.cengage.com/region**

Visit National Geographic Learning online at **NGL.Cengage.com/ELT**
Visit our corporate website at **www.cengage.com**

Printed in the United States of America

Print Number: 01   Print Year: 2017

TABLE OF CONTENTS

TEACHING WITH *PATHWAYS*

In *Pathways Listening, Speaking, and Critical Thinking, Second Edition*, real-world content from National Geographic provides a context for meaningful language acquisition. Each unit's authentic, relevant, and high-interest content is designed to motivate both students and teachers alike. Students will learn essential vocabulary, review important grammatical structures, and practice listening and speaking skills that will allow them to succeed in academic settings.

Each unit of *Pathways Listening, Speaking, and Critical Thinking* features:

- Academic Skills objectives listed at the start of each unit.
- Explore the Theme pages that introduce the unit theme while developing visual literacy skills.
- Target vocabulary presented in interesting and varied contexts.
- Extensive audio program including lectures, interviews, conversations, podcasts, and pronunciation models that expose students to different genres and speakers.
- Skills boxes that instruct students on key vocabulary, listening, note-taking, speaking, pronunciation, grammar, and presentation skills.
- A Critical Thinking focus in every unit, in addition to activities that practice a variety of critical thinking skills.
- Lesson and Final Tasks that get students to synthesize language, skills, and content, and to apply this knowledge to topics of interest to them.
- A Reflection section that encourages students to reflect on what they have learned.

The *Pathways* series is flexible and designed to be used in a wide variety of language-learning programs, from high schools and community colleges, to private language institutes and intensive English programs. A Pacing Guide for implementing the program in various teaching situations is provided on page xii. In addition to the student book, the *Pathways* series offers an Online Workbook where students can get extra listening practice with additional audio, watch the National Geographic videos, and work on 20 additional activities per unit that reinforce the skills introduced in the book.

Teaching Academic Literacy

In addition to teaching essential listening and speaking skills, the *Pathways* series promotes other aspects of academic literacy that will help students succeed in an academic setting, such as:

- visual literacy;
- critical thinking;
- collaboration skills;
- presentation skills;
- digital literacy.

Students build essential academic literacy skills while encountering fascinating stories about real people and places around the world. The use of informative, relevant, and authoritative content from National Geographic builds global and cultural awareness, and develops learners' understanding of important 21st century issues that affect us all. While these skills are components of academic literacy, they will also serve students in their work lives as well.

Increasing Visual Literacy

Photographs, maps, charts, and graphs can all convey enormous amounts of information, and it is essential for students to be able to make sense of them. *Pathways* uses high quality visuals to help students develop the ability to interpret and discuss visual information.

STIMULATING INFOGRAPHICS from National Geographic publications help explain complex processes.

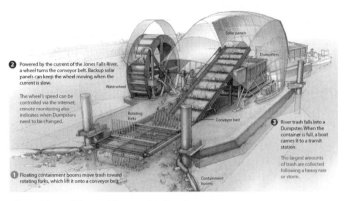

©Bruce Morser/National Geographic Creative

CHARTS AND GRAPHS present numerical information visually.

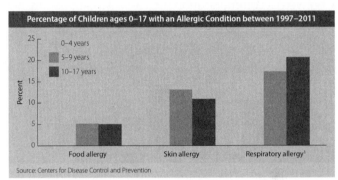

MAPS show locations and geographical features, and illustrate historical facts and current trends.

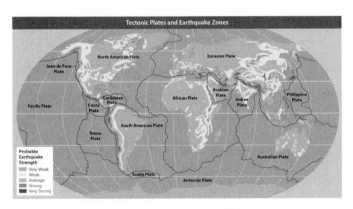

"The Geography of Transport Systems" https://people.hofstra. edu/geotrans /eng/ch9en/conc9en/plate_tectonics.html

GRAPHIC ORGANIZERS show the relationships between ideas.

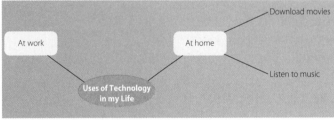

Using Videos

Pathways uses videos from National Geographic's award-winning film collection. They present a unique and visually dynamic perspective on the unit theme.

Teaching Video-Viewing Skills

Videos differ from listening passages in important ways. Because students are processing more than just words, extra layers of meaning need to be understood, such as:

- information about the video's setting;
- signs and captions identifying people or places;
- maps and diagrams explaining information and processes;
- nonverbal communication such as facial expressions, gestures, and body language;
- music and sound effects.

All *Pathways* videos come with the option to use English subtitles, and with full English transcripts that can be found at the end of this teacher's guide.

The Video Section

Each unit features activities for students to do *before, while*, and *after* watching the video.

BEFORE VIEWING

This section provides background knowledge and stimulates interest in the topic. Activities include:

- pre-teaching vocabulary from the video;
- providing background information about the topic;
- predicting video content using images and captions.

WHILE VIEWING

As they watch the video, students complete activities such as:

- checking their predictions;
- identifying main ideas;
- watching and listening for details;
- inferring opinions and attitudes.

AFTER VIEWING

Students check comprehension and relate the video to other aspects of the unit and their own lives by completing activities such as:

- analyzing the sequence of events in the video;
- applying the ideas in the videos to their communities;
- synthesizing information from the video and information from the listening passage.

Building Critical Thinking Skills

Students today are expected to do more than just learn and memorize information. The ability to think critically about a topic—to analyze, apply, and evaluate ideas—is increasingly essential in an academic setting. *Pathways* actively fosters critical thinking while students complete listening and speaking activities.

Critical Thinking and Language

Critical thinking requires a deep processing of language, which aids in language acquisition. Articulating complex responses requires creative thought and word associations, which lead to better comprehension and retention of target language.

These are some of the critical thinking skills covered in *Pathways*:

- **Analyzing** a passage in close detail in order to identify key points, similarities, and differences.
- **Applying** information to a different context e.g., applying possible solutions to problems.
- **Evaluating** how relevant, important, or useful something is. This involves, for example, looking carefully at the sources of information, or the reasons the speaker provides for or against something.
- **Inferring** what a speaker is saying indirectly, or implicitly, rather than directly, or explicitly.
- **Synthesizing** appropriate information and ideas from more than one source to make a judgment, summary, or conclusion based on the evidence.
- **Reflecting** on ideas and information in a text in order to relate them to your own personal experience and viewpoints, and to form your own opinion.

While each unit contains several opportunities for critical thinking, there is also a Critical Thinking Focus in every unit:

> **CRITICAL THINKING**   Synthesizing
>
> When you synthesize, you combine, or put together, information from two or more sources in order to understand a topic in a new way. This can also involve combining new information with your own ideas and knowledge about a topic. Synthesizing can help you find a solution to a problem or think of new ways of doing or improving something.

Preparing for Standardized Tests

Pathways is designed to provide practice for standardized exams, such as IELTS and TOEFL. Many activities practice or focus on key exam skills needed for test success. In the student book you will find an index of activities that are similar to common question types found in these tests.

Frequently Asked Questions

How are the Student Book units organized?

Foundations includes eight units, while levels 1-4 each include 10 units.

Each unit consists of seven main sections:

Vocabulary A, Listening A, Speaking A, Video, Vocabulary B, Listening B, and Speaking B

The unit opens with an introduction to the unit theme. The listening passages and videos that follow, together with their corresponding exercises, then build towards a final speaking task that synthesizes the skills, topics, and language presented in the unit.

Will my students be able to handle the themes in the book?

The content and language are graded so that students can come into the series with little or no background information.

Each unit starts with a Think and Discuss page. This consists of a compelling photograph and questions designed to spark students' curiosity about the theme. The Explore the Theme spread further engages students and taps into their critical thinking with a thought-provoking angle on the theme presented through photos, text, and infographics.

As students progress through a unit, exercises and activities further add to students' knowledge of the theme. So, by the time students get to the final speaking task, they have enough language and information to speak with confidence about the topic.

How are Listenings A and B related?

The two listenings offer different perspectives on the unit theme. They consist of contrasting listening types, for example, one might be a lecture by a university professor, and the other a conversation among students. The variety of listening passages is designed to mirror the range that learners will encounter in academic and real-world settings.

How does the series build vocabulary skills?

Each listening passage contains ten high-frequency vocabulary items (eight in *Foundations)*. These are introduced in the Vocabulary sections, which focus on developing students' ability to use contextual clues to determine meaning. Target words are then reinforced and recycled throughout the series.

How are listening and speaking integrated in the series?

All of the sections and exercises in each unit are thematically linked. Listenings A and B and their corresponding activities present and reinforce ideas, vocabulary, and grammar that students will use in their Speaking activities. For example, students may learn to listen for problems and solutions in the Listening section, and then role-play a conversation in which they analyze problems and offer solutions in the final speaking task. Or students may hear about explorers in a listening passage, and then be asked to talk about a place they would like to explore.

How does *Pathways* develop listening and speaking skills?

Each unit of *Pathways Listening, Speaking, and Critical Thinking* contains two listening sections. The language in the listening passages represents realistic situations, yet the language is controlled for level, and students may listen to each passage more than once. This guided listening gives students the chance to practice listening and note-taking skills and to develop the confidence and fluency they'll need before they are immersed in an academic setting.

Each Listening section contains three parts:

- Before Listening activities provide background information and explicit instruction in listening skills.
- While Listening activities give students practice in listening for main ideas and details, and in making inferences.
- After Listening activities are designed to reinforce listening skills by allowing students to discuss and react to the listening passage.

Every section of *Pathways Listening, Speaking, and Critical Thinking* provides opportunities for classroom speaking and discussion, often in pairs or in small groups. Frequent classroom discussions and interactions prepare students to participate in class and succeed in an academic setting. In the Speaking sections, striking images and brief stories about real people and places often provide the content for engaging interactions. Speaking activities are designed with a scaffolded approach. They progress from controlled and guided activities to more open and communicative activities. Early confidence-building motivates students to attempt activities that increase in difficulty, taking them to their ultimate goal—participation in authentic speaking activities such as classroom presentations, formal discussions, and debates.

The Speaking sections contain:

- Clear and succinct grammar boxes which give students a single language structure to concentrate on. The grammar points lend themselves to discussion of the unit theme and can be recycled throughout the unit.
- A Presentation Skill box at points where students give presentations, so they provide immediate practice of skills needed for planning and delivering successful oral presentations.
- An Everyday Language box that provides tips and expressions to help students develop the language they will need for class work and in their day-to-day exchanges.
- A Speaking Task. The Lesson Task and Final Task are consolidating speaking activities. They often involve collaboration with a partner or a group as well as an oral presentation of results or ideas.

The *MyELT* online workbook provides additional guided listening and speaking tasks that build on the skills and language learners have developed in the Student Book unit.

How does the *Listening, Speaking, and Critical Thinking* strand align with the *Reading, Writing, and Critical Thinking* strand?

The content in each unit is related to the content in the corresponding strand. For example, in level 1, Unit 3, "The Marketing Machine," students learn about business and marketing in the *Listening and Speaking* strand, and about the same academic track in "Why We Buy" in level 1, Unit 3 of the *Reading and Writing* strand. Language has also been controlled and recycled so that students meet similar structures and vocabulary across the two strands.

SPEAKING ASSESSMENT RUBRIC

Rating	General Description	Pronunciation & Fluency	Vocabulary	Topic Development
4	The student speaks smoothly and effectively, similar to a native speaker.	The student's pronunciation is similar to a native speaker's. S/he speaks clearly and articulately with little or no hesitation.	The student's vocabulary is sophisticated and similar to a native speaker's.	The student's content reflects a deep understanding of the topic.
3	The student can express him/herself with relative ease and fluency and very few errors.	The student's pronunciation is clear, with few errors. S/he is able to respond to the prompt with relative ease.	The student's vocabulary enhances his or her response to the prompt.	The student's content is relevant to the topic and shows a good understanding.
2	The student is generally able to make him/herself understood, with some hesitation and errors.	The student is inconsistent in his or her pronunciation. The student demonstrates some fluency and is able to put together simple sentences.	The student's vocabulary relates to the topic, but is basic and with a few errors.	The student's content has some relevance to the topic, but is not well developed.
1	The student's response is very limited in content &/or coherence.	The student struggles to pronounce words and has difficulty putting words together to form a sentence.	The student's vocabulary is limited to high frequency words.	The student's content is minimally relevant to the topic or prompt.
0	The student does not respond, or the response is unrelated to the prompt.			

USING THE TEACHER'S GUIDE

Each unit of this Teacher's Guide contains:

- A list of the academic skills covered in the unit.
- An overview of the unit theme, the listening passages, the video, and the Final Task.
- Suggestions for online search terms for additional information about topics in the unit.
- Teaching notes for each exercise.
- Answer keys.

Other features include:

Recommended Time Frames

Look for the small clock icon with recommended times for completing various tasks. While the recommended total time required for each unit is about six class hours, this will of course vary depending on your particular teaching situation. Likewise, the time allocated for specific sections should be used more as a guide than as a rule. Refer to the Pacing Guide on the following page for a more detailed breakdown.

Ideas for…EXPANSION

These boxes contain suggestions for extra classroom activities that can be used when students need additional support, have a high level of interest in the topic, or when there is an opportunity to explore a different aspect of the unit theme.

Ideas for…PRESENTING THE SKILL

These boxes provide a variety of ways to introduce the skill being taught as well as practical suggestions for quick activities to put the skill in use.

Ideas for…CHECKING COMPREHENSION

These boxes offer additional suggestions for assessing students' comprehension during class and provide exercises to check for understanding.

Ideas for…MULTI-LEVEL CLASSES

These boxes provide techniques for use in mixed-ability classrooms, where learner diversity can benefit everyone in the class.

TIPS

These supplementary teaching tips are general suggestions to facilitate classroom management, such as asking student volunteers to record answers on the board as you lead a discussion.

In addition, this teacher's guide also contains *Audio Scripts* and *Video Scripts*, which can be found at the back of this book.

Use these for a more detailed study of the audio and video content. The scripts, for example, can be provided to students for additional comprehension practice before or after they listen to the passage or view the video.

PACING GUIDE

One unit of *Pathways Listening, Speaking, and Critical Thinking* typically requires six hours to complete. If you have limited class time, we recommend focusing on Speaking activities in class and assigning Vocabulary, Video, and/or Listening activities as independent work. By setting aside some of these activities as homework, or by using expansion activities and the Online Workbook, a *Pathways* unit can be adapted to suit various course durations:

Total course length: 45 hours	Total course length: 60 hours	Total course length: 90 hours	Total course length: 120 hours
30-week course: 1 × 90 minute class per week 1 unit = 3 classes (4.5 classroom hours)	**30-Week Course:** 2 × 60 min classes per week **15-Week Course:** 4 × 60 min classes per week 1 unit = 6 classes (6 classroom hours)	**30-Week Course:** 2 × 90 min classes per week 1 unit = 5 classes (7.5 classroom hours)	**30-Week Course:** 4 × 60 min classes per week 1 unit = 8 classes (8 classroom hours)
This plan assumes that: – The Vocabulary activities are assigned as homework and reviewed in class. – Listening B is assigned as homework through the Online Workbook and reviewed in class.	This plan assumes that there is enough time to complete the entire student book in class. To make time for expansion activities: – The Vocabulary activities can be assigned as homework and reviewed in class. – Online Workbook activities can be done in a lab setting.	This plan assumes that there is enough time to complete the entire student book in class. – Some follow-up questions and expansion activities in the Teacher's Guide can be used. – Online Workbook activities can be done in a lab setting. – ExamView unit tests can be done in class.	This plan assumes that there is enough time to complete the entire student book in class. – More follow-up questions and expansion activities in the Teacher's Guide can be used. – Online Workbook activities can be done in a lab setting. – ExamView unit tests can be done in class.
Class 1: Think and Discuss Explore the Theme A: Vocabulary A: Listening **Class 2:** A: Speaking Lesson Task Video **Class 3:** B: Vocabulary B: Listening B: Speaking Final Task Reflection	**Class 1:** Think and Discuss Explore the Theme A: Vocabulary **Class 2:** A: Listening **Class 3:** A: Speaking Lesson Task **Class 4:** Video B: Vocabulary **Class 5:** B: Listening B: Speaking **Class 6:** Final Task Reflection	**Class 1:** Think and Discuss Explore the Theme A: Vocabulary **Class 2:** A: Listening A: Speaking **Class 3:** Lesson Task Video **Class 4:** B: Vocabulary B: Listening **Class 5:** B: Speaking Final Task Reflection	**Class 1:** Think and Discuss Explore the Theme A: Vocabulary **Class 2:** A: Listening **Class 3:** A: Speaking Lesson Task **Class 4:** Video **Class 5:** B: Vocabulary B: Listening **Class 6:** B: Speaking **Class 7:** Final Task Reflection **Class 8:** Expansion activities / group projects

HEALTHY LIVES

ACADEMIC TRACK
Health Science

ACADEMIC SKILLS

LISTENING	Listening for Main Ideas
	Writing Key Words and Phrases
SPEAKING	Keeping a Conversation Going
	Final -s Sounds
CRITICAL THINKING	Interpreting Visuals

UNIT OVERVIEW

Staying healthy is important to everyone, regardless of age. The theme of this unit is how people around the world are fighting against modern-day diseases with innovation, education, alternative medicine, and tried-and-true healthy lifestyle habits.

- **LISTENING A A Talk about Preventing Heart Disease:** A public health nurse gives a talk about habits and lifestyle choices that can help prevent heart disease.

- **VIDEO *Bee Therapy*:** Although it seems painful and unpleasant, some people have found that bee sting therapy has a positive effect on certain illnesses such as arthritis and multiple sclerosis.

- **LISTENING B A Conversation about Allergies:** Two students have a conversation about the causes of allergies and the fact that they are becoming increasingly common.

For the final task, students draw upon what they have learned in the unit to participate in a group discussion about health. As a group, students choose one of three topics and have a 4-5-minute discussion about it.

For additional information about the topics in this unit, here are some suggestions for online search terms: *World Health Organization, public health nurses, heart disease, treadmill desk, bee therapy, honeybees, traditional medicine, modern medicine, allergies, asthma, acupuncture*

 **UNIT OPENER**

THINK AND DISCUSS   *(page 1)*

Direct students' attention to the photo, title, and caption. Ask leading questions, such as:
- Who is the woman in the picture? (*an athlete, or just someone interested in staying healthy and fit*)
- Where is she? (*at a stadium*)

ANSWER KEY

THINK AND DISCUSS *(page 1)*

1. Possible answers: She's running up stadium stairs. She may be preparing for a race or other event, or just exercising.
2. Answers will vary.

EXPLORE THE THEME   *(pages 2–3)*

In small groups, have students look at the world map, describe the photos, read the captions, and discuss the questions. Ask volunteers to share any personal experiences with friends or family members who have lived long, healthy lives.

ANSWER KEY

EXPLORE THE THEME *(pages 2–3)*

1. Possible answers: The man in Costa Rica probably eats a lot of fruits and vegetables. The man and woman in Italy probably get a lot of exercise. The man in Japan probably finds ways to relax and have fun. The husband and wife in Greece probably spend time with each other, friends, and family.
2. Answers will vary.
3. Possible answers: Not smoke; exercise; get enough sleep
4. Answers will vary.

Lesson A

⏱ **VOCABULARY** *30 MINS*

A **Meaning from Context** *(page 4)*

Have students work in pairs as they read the sentences aloud and predict meaning.

B 🎧 **1.2** *(page 4)*

Play the audio twice, if necessary.

> **Ideas for… CHECKING COMPREHENSION**
>
> Help students summarize the main ideas in the text by asking them to complete these sentences:
> 1. *In Sardinia, men live longer because…*
> 2. *In Okinawa, people live longer because…*

C *(page 4)*

Ask volunteers to read sentences from exercise A aloud as you go over the answers. Have students identify the context clues that helped them choose the correct word for each definition.

D *(page 5)*

Have students work individually to complete the exercise. Remind them to pay attention to the parts of speech. Have them form pairs and compare answers.

E **Critical Thinking: Reflecting** *(page 5)*

Discuss answers as a class. Write students' ideas for number 4 on the board. Have the class rank the habits in order of how healthy they are, with 1 being the healthiest.

F **Personalizing** *(page 5)*

As a review, have volunteers read questions aloud. Take a class poll for each question, eliciting students' responses and writing how many students responded *yes* and *no* for each question on the board. Ask students to analyze how many of them are likely to live to be 100 and why.

 LISTENING: A TALK ABOUT PREVENTING HEART DISEASE *45 MINS*

BEFORE LISTENING

A 🎧 **1.3** *(page 6)*

Read the information and statements together as a class before listening to the talk.

> **Ideas for… CHECKING COMPREHENSION**
>
> Check students' understanding of what public health nurses do by asking the following questions:
> • How are public health nurses different from other nurses? (*Most nurses care for one patient at a time; public health nurses care for entire populations.*)
> • Who are their patients? (*many different groups of people, including children, teens, and adults of all ages*)
> • Where do they work? (*hospitals, clinics, schools*)
> • Would you like to be a public health nurse? Why or why not?

B **Predicting** *(page 6)*

Go over the topics in the box before discussing them. Answer any questions about meaning or use.

WHILE LISTENING

C 🎧 1.4 Checking Predictions *(page 6)*

Review the topics the nurse includes in her talk. Ask students how many topics they predicted accurately.

> **Ideas for... PRESENTING THE LISTENING SKILL:** Listening for Main Ideas
>
> Reinforce the concept of main idea versus details by showing students photos of events, such as a football game, a wedding, or a doctor's visit. On the board, make a T-chart with the heading *Main idea* in the left column and *Details* in the right. Show the first picture and ask "What is the main idea of this picture?" Have students guess and write ideas in the left column. Then ask "How did you know the main idea?" As students describe what's going on in the photo, write those details in the right column. Repeat this exercise with additional photos.

TIP Whenever possible, ask student volunteers to record answers on the board as you lead a class discussion.

D 🎧 1.4 ▶ 1.1 Listening for Main Ideas
(page 7)

Check answers as a class. Ask students which technique from the *Listening Skill* box they used to identify the main ideas.

E 🎧 1.4 Listening for Details *(page 7)*

Give students time to read through the questions and answers before they listen to the audio again. Ask volunteers to read their answers aloud and explain the reasons for their choices.

AFTER LISTENING

F Critical Thinking: Reflecting *(page 7)*

Ask volunteers which of the nurse's suggestions are most likely to help prevent heart disease and why. Be sure they give reasons for their opinions.

> **Ideas for... EXPANSION**
>
> In small groups, have students make an informational brochure or fact sheet on preventing heart disease. Ask them to include only main ideas and present the information in a visual way. Have each group present its brochure to another small group.

ANSWER KEY

LISTENING

A *(page 6)* **1.** T; **2.** T; **3.** T; **4.** F (It will be about heart disease and how to prevent it.)

B *(page 6)* Answers will vary.

C *(page 6)* The nurse includes the following in her talk: attitude (in relation to dealing with stress), blood pressure, diet, exercise, smoking, and stress

D *(page 7)*

1. Get your blood pressure checked. Deal with stress in healthy ways. Eat a healthy diet. Get enough exercise. Quit smoking.

2. high blood pressure; smoking; high blood sugar

E *(page 7)* **1.** a; **2.** b; **3.** a

F *(page 7)* Answers will vary.

SPEAKING

Ideas for... PRESENTING PRONUNCIATION: Final -s Sounds

🎧 1.5 Exaggerate the -s sound and syllables as you read the examples in the box aloud.

A 🎧 1.6 *(page 8)*

Have students tap out the number of syllables in each target word on their desks or tables as they listen. Ask them to identify the target words in which the -s or -es ending adds a syllable.

B *(page 8)*

Elicit additional examples from students of words that end in -s or -es. Write the examples on the board, and have volunteers read the words aloud to practice pronunciation.

Ideas for... PRESENTING GRAMMAR FOR SPEAKING: Expressions of Frequency

Explain that the word *frequency* refers to the number of times something happens during a particular period. For practice in the use of correct word order with expressions of frequency, read aloud some sentence starters without expressions of frequency (such as *I play soccer…, I am too busy to go to the gym…, I go to the dentist…, I take a vacation…*), and ask students to write them down and add an expression of frequency so the sentences are true for them. Then ask volunteers to read their sentences aloud and determine whether the word order is correct.

C Personalizing *(page 9)*

Have students work with different partners for exercises C and D.

TIP At the beginning of a course, it's important for students to get to know each other. Have students change partners often so that they work with different classmates.

Ideas for... EXPANSION

Have students add to the list in their book by writing five more questions beginning with "How often do you…" Then ask them to stand up and mingle with classmates. For each question, each student should find a new partner. Partners should take turns asking and answering one of the questions. Encourage them to ask follow-up questions to develop fluency.

D Critical Thinking: Analyzing *(page 9)*

Ask volunteers to write their advice from question 4 on the board. As a class, check the sentences for correct word order, use of modal auxiliaries, subject-verb agreement, and expressions of frequency.

Ideas for... EXPANSION

Have each student find a partner and role-play a doctor's visit. Partner A is the patient and should explain his or her concerns about heart disease. Partner B is the doctor and should give at least five suggestions on how to prevent heart disease. Give them a couple of minutes to decide on roles and 5 to 10 minutes to complete the activity. Encourage students to look at their notes from exercise D as they role-play. Have volunteers act out a doctor's visit in front of the class.

Critical Thinking: Applying *(page 10)*

Arrange students in groups of three. Walk around the class, monitoring their work.

F *(page 10)*

If necessary, give students time to write their findings as notes they can use when they present them.

TIP Keep in mind that not all students will have an exercise routine to discuss. Some students may not like exercising or may be unable to participate in physical activity because of a disability. In this case, ask these students what other kinds of activities they enjoy, and emphasize to the class the importance of differences.

ANSWER KEY

SPEAKING

A *(page 8)*

1. Frank <u>exercises</u> (4) every day. He <u>plays</u> (1) <u>sports</u> (1) and <u>lifts</u> (1) <u>weights</u> (1)

2. There are 16 <u>doctors</u> (2) and 37 <u>nurses</u> (2) at the hospital.

3. I eat <u>pears</u> (1), <u>peaches</u> (2), and other <u>kinds</u> (1) of fruit almost every day.

4. Stress <u>causes</u> (2) a lot of health <u>problems</u> (2).

5. The yoga class <u>begins</u> (2) when the teacher <u>closes</u> (2) the door.

B–C *(pages 8–9)* Answers will vary.

D *(page 9)*

1. He is walking on a treadmill while he is working.

2. Possible answer: It can help him deal with stress and prevent heart disease.

3. Answers will vary.

4. Possible answers: Everyone should exercise at least three times a week. You should stand up and walk every hour while you are working at a desk.

E–F *(page 10)* Answers will vary.

 **LESSON TASK: PRESENTING HEALTHY HABITS**

A 🎧 **1.7** *(page 11)*

Before listening to the talk, have students preview the four parts of the presentation. Afterward, have them discuss in pairs what information was included in each part. For example, in the introduction, the speaker greeted the audience and said her name.

B **Organizing Ideas** *(page 11)*

Conduct a class brainstorming session on transition words and phrases, and write ideas on the board. Remind students to use this vocabulary to link the ideas in their presentation.

> **Ideas for… PRESENTING THE PRESENTATION SKILL:** Practicing Your Presentation
>
> Teach students how to give effective feedback. Suggest that they include what their partner did well, what he or she needs to work on, and what steps he or she can take to improve. Remind students that simple and specific feedback is most helpful.

C *(page 11)*

Give students time for each partner to practice at least twice. While they are practicing, walk around the classroom, and offer help and advice as needed.

> **Ideas for… MULTI-LEVEL CLASSES**
>
> Encourage students to practice with their answers from exercise B and present them without notes. However, to help increase their confidence, lower-level students could practice with a script and use notes when they give their presentations. In this case, demonstrate the difference between reading from notes and just glancing at notes at strategic moments during a speech.

D **Presenting** *(page 11)*

If possible, aim to leave 3 to 5 minutes for follow-up questions after each student's presentation.

ANSWER KEY

LESSON TASK

A *(page 11)* All boxes should be checked.

B–D *(page 11)* Answers will vary.

Video

45 MINS **VIEWING:** *BEE THERAPY* *(page 12)*

Overview of the Video

Although it seems painful and unpleasant, some people have found that bee sting therapy has a positive effect on certain illnesses such as arthritis and multiple sclerosis.

BEFORE VIEWING

A **Personalizing** *(page 12)*

Ask students to look at the photo and share what they know about bees. Ask "How do you think bee therapy works? What kinds of diseases might it treat?"

B *(page 12)*

Ask students which words they already know. Ask them in what contexts they have heard them used.

C **Prior Knowledge** *(page 13)*

Ask students to read the information and ask questions about these diseases. On the board, make a list of some questions students have about these diseases.

WHILE VIEWING

D ▶ 1.2 **Understanding Main Ideas** *(page 13)*

Point out that only Mr. Chen and Mr. Chen's wife are related, even though all three people have the same name.

E ▶ 1.2 **Understanding Details** *(page 13)*

Give students time to read through the questions before they watch the video again. Make sure students know what type of information is required.

AFTER VIEWING

F **Critical Thinking: Reflecting** *(page 13)*

Have volunteers share traditional or natural remedies they know about with the class.

ANSWER KEY

VIDEO

A *(page 12)*

  1.–2. Answers will vary.

  3. Possible answer: Traditional medicine may work better for small problems, and modern medicine may work better for serious diseases.

B *(page 12)* **1.** c; **2.** d; **3.** e; **4.** b; **5.** a

C *(page 13)* Answers will vary.

D *(page 13)* **a.** 3; **b.** 2; **c.** 1

E *(page 13)* **1.** 200, 6000; **2.** 600, 5; **3.** 5000; **4.** 3; **5.** 6

F *(page 13)* Answers will vary.

Lesson B

⏱30 MINS VOCABULARY

A 🎧 1.8 Meaning from Context (page 14)

Ask students what they know about allergies. Play the audio while students read along. Ask them to describe the diagram after they have read the text.

B (page 14)

Have students complete the exercise individually and check answers in pairs.

> **Ideas for... PRESENTING THE VOCABULARY SKILL:** Understanding Meaning from Context
>
> Read the example aloud and point out the context clues that help define the word *reaction*. Have students return to the text and check the meanings of the words *immune system, pollen, antibodies, sneezing,* and *itching*. Ask them what context clues they used to determine the meanings of the words.

C 🎧 1.9 Meaning from Context (page 15)

Explain that the word *hygiene* means the things that you do to keep yourself and your surroundings clean to maintain good health. Elicit examples of good and poor hygiene from the class.

> **Ideas for... EXPANSION**
>
> Have students form pairs and share their backgrounds and views about the hygiene hypothesis. Ask "Did you grow up in a really clean house? Do you agree with the hygiene hypothesis? Why or why not?" Remind them to give specific reasons for their opinions.

ANSWER KEY

VOCABULARY

B (page 14) **1.** cell; **2.** attach; **3.** produces; **4.** responds; **5.** defends; **6.** occurs

C (page 15) **1.** contains; **2.** common; **3.** research; **4.** theory

⏱45 MINS LISTENING: A CONVERSATION ABOUT ALLERGIES

BEFORE LISTENING

A (page 16)

Ask two volunteers to read the conversation aloud. Have volunteers share whether they or someone they know has a food allergy and what it is like.

WHILE LISTENING

B 🎧 1.10 Listening for Main Ideas (page 16)

Point out that students should listen for the topics that the speakers are *most* concerned about, not just which topics are mentioned.

> **Ideas for... PRESENTING THE NOTE-TAKING SKILL:** Taking Notes on Key Words and Phrases
>
> Tell students to identify key words and phrases by listening for the words in each sentence that convey the most information and receive the most stress. Remind them that they may need to listen to the sentences more than once to distinguish which words they should write down.

C 🎧 1.10 Note Taking (page 16)

Read the questions aloud and ask students whether they can answer any of them before playing the audio again.

AFTER LISTENING

D Critical Thinking: Interpreting a Bar Graph (page 17)

Before discussing, have students look at the graph and point to the title, the legend, and the two axes.

E Personalizing (page 17)

As a review, have students share their opinions about food policies. As a class, brainstorm reasons for and against food policies in organizations. Write reasons on the board, and have volunteers take sides and participate in debate.

LISTENING

A *(page 16)* Possible answers:

1. She's surprised that the body responds in the same way to different allergies.
2. Because it might cause serious reactions such as difficulty breathing.

B *(page 16)*

✓ asthma

✓ food allergies

C *(page 16)*

1. spring + early summer
2. air pollution + plants
3. no peanuts
4. 1997–2011
5. 7%–8%

D *(page 17)*

1. percentage of children ages 0–17 with an allergic condition between 1997–2011
2. The vertical axis shows the percentage of children with an allergy; the horizontal axis shows the type of allergy.
3. the percentage of children between 0–4 years
4. skin allergies
5. children 10–17 years old
6. respiratory allergies
7. food allergies
8. 5%

E *(page 17)* Answers will vary.

SPEAKING

Ideas for… PRESENTING THE SPEAKING SKILL: Keeping a Conversation Going

Read through the information provided in the box with students. Elicit examples of the three different ways to keep a conversation going. Write ideas on the board for reference as students are having their conversations.

Ideas for… EXPANSION

Ask students whether they think it is appropriate to ask people about personal experiences in a workplace or business setting. Have them share their opinions with classmates from different cultures and backgrounds.

A *(page 18)*

Before practicing, have students underline any expressions of interest, follow-up questions, or *wh-*questions.

B **Keeping a Conversation Going** *(page 18)*

Ideas for… EXPANSION

Ask students to imagine they are at a dinner party. Play some soft music, and ask them to walk around the classroom. When you stop the music, mention one of the topics in the box. Students should stop walking and start a conversation with the classmates near them about this topic. After 2 minutes, play the music again and repeat the process.

SPEAKING

B *(page 18)* Answers will vary.

FINAL TASK: PARTICIPATING IN A DISCUSSION ABOUT HEALTH

A *(page 19)*

Give groups time to read the information about group discussions. Review the topic choices in the chart.

Ideas for... CHECKING COMPREHENSION

Check students' understanding by asking the following questions:

- What are different ways to participate in a discussion? *(contributing ideas, keeping discussion going)*
- How can your group make sure every member has an opportunity to speak? *(pay attention to each other and show interest)*
- What are some tips to speak clearly? *(higher volume, slower pace)*
- Who in the group will be the note taker?

B Organizing Ideas *(page 19)*

Have students brainstorm and take notes individually before they participate in the discussion.

C Critical Thinking: Applying *(page 20)*

Keep track of the time, and walk around the classroom to monitor group work.

D Critical Thinking: Reflecting *(page 20)*

Have students do a quick free writing exercise to answer questions 1 through 4. Remind them that they do not need to worry about grammar or consult a dictionary; the idea is to reflect on and explore their feelings before discussing them with their group.

TIP Consider assigning roles to all groups members to increase participation. In addition to having a recorder take notes on the discussion, you could have a group leader to keep the conversation on track, a time keeper, and a reporter to use the recorder's notes to report to the whole class.

ANSWER KEY

FINAL TASK

A–D *(pages 19-20)* Answers will vary.

REFLECTION

- Have students answer questions 1 and 2 on their own, and then discuss their answers in pairs or small groups.
- Ask students to discuss similarities and differences in their answers for questions 1 and 2.
- For question 3, have students compare answers and then write the words about which they are still unsure on the board. Lead a class review of the challenging words, and teach terms again as necessary.

TECHNOLOGY TODAY AND TOMORROW

ACADEMIC TRACK
Technology

ACADEMIC SKILLS

LISTENING	Identifying Important Details
	Using Abbreviations
SPEAKING	Giving Reasons
	Stressed Content Words
CRITICAL THINKING	Synthesizing

UNIT OVERVIEW

The theme of this unit is how people all over the world are using technology to solve everyday problems and how new technological advances and innovations will continue to change how people live and work in the future.

- **LISTENING A A Radio Show about AI:** A radio show host interviews a doctor about the role that artificial intelligence plays in our daily lives and how it might be used in the future.

- **VIDEO *Can Robots Learn to Be More Human?*:** National Geographic Explorer, computer scientist, and robotics expert Chad Jenkins explains how coming breakthroughs in robotics will soon make robots a bigger part of everyday life, helping us perform more tasks in our homes and workplaces.

- **LISTENING B A Conversation about Technology:** Two friends have a conversation about the benefits and the kinds of technology involved in Baltimore's "Mr. Trash Wheel." The trash wheel uses the movement of the Jones Falls River along with solar energy to remove trash from the water before it reaches the Atlantic Ocean.

For the final task, students draw upon what they have learned in the unit to give a pair presentation about a new kind of technology that will help solve a problem that they have identified.

For additional information about the topics in this unit, here are some suggestions for online search terms: *Pokémon Go, artificial intelligence, 2001: A Space Odyssey, science fiction, Isaac Asimov, early computers, robots, search engines, smartphones, self-driving cars, computer coding, remote presence device, climate change, fossil fuels, renewable energy, solar power, wind power, Mr. Trash Wheel, Baltimore Maryland, Jones Falls River*

20 MINS UNIT OPENER

THINK AND DISCUSS *(page 21)*

Direct students' attention to the photo, title, and caption. Ask leading questions, such as:
- Who are the people in the picture? *(mostly teenagers and young adults; millennials)*
- Where are they? *(at La Villette park in Paris, France)*

ANSWER KEY

THINK AND DISCUSS *(page 21)*
1. They are in groups of friends playing Pokémon Go on their cell phones. Other answers will vary.
2. The title is *Technology Today and Tomorrow*. Other answers will vary.

EXPLORE THE THEME *(pages 22–23)*

- Ask a volunteer to read the *Explore the Theme* title and description aloud.
- In small groups, have students describe the photos, read the timeline entries, and discuss the questions.
- Review answers as a class. Ask students what else they would like to know about artificial intelligence (AI).

ANSWER KEY

EXPLORE THE THEME *(pages 22–23)*
1. Answers will vary.
2. They felt AI was dangerous. They were afraid of it. Other answers will vary.
3. Answers will vary.
4. Possible answer: AI may make our lives easier. It may help us clean our houses, improve our health, and give us more entertainment.

Lesson A

VOCABULARY
30 MINS

A 🎧 1.11 **Meaning from Context** *(page 24)*

Have students analyze the timeline before listening to the information. Ask them the following questions to check their understanding of how the timeline presents information:

- What type of information does the timeline present? *(important events in AI history)*
- How does it present this information? *(on a vertical line with specific intervals shown chronologically)*
- How long is each specific interval? *(10 years)*
- How many important events are presented? *(six)*
- How many years are represented on the timeline? *(70)*

B *(page 25)*

Have students work in pairs. Remind them to use context to work out the meanings of the words in blue.

C *(page 25)*

Have volunteers share their answers for questions 1 to 3 with the class.

D *(page 25)*

Point out the parts of speech to students. Make sure they understand what each abbreviation means and that the parts of speech describe how each word is used in exercise A.

Ideas for… PRESENTING THE VOCABULARY SKILL: Using Collocations

Have students look at the text in exercise A and underline any collocations they find. Examples are *depending on* and *an important part of*. Throughout the unit, continue to call students' attention to collocations and have them underline these common phrases in their textbooks for future reference.

E **Critical Thinking: Analyzing** *(page 25)*

After students identify the collocations and answer the questions in a group, ask them to form new sentences using the collocations.

LISTENING: A RADIO SHOW ABOUT AI
45 MINS

BEFORE LISTENING

A **Prior Knowledge** *(page 26)*

If possible, pull up search engines or online shopping sites as students share answers.

TIP Create a high context learning space by incorporating visuals, videos, music, and movement whenever possible. A variety of stimuli will activate background knowledge and increase learning.

WHILE LISTENING

Ideas for… EXPANSION

Have students form pairs and cover the caption for the image and guess what it says. Ask "Who are these people? Where are they? What are they doing? How does this photo relate to the listening and the theme of the unit?"

B 🎧 1.12 **Listening for Main Ideas** *(page 26)*

Tell students they will listen to a talk radio interview about AI between a host and a guest expert. Have students review the questions and answer choices before they listen to the interview.

TIP Briefly introduce students to the concept of talk radio. Explain that many radio stations broadcast shows, hosted by an individual, that feature guest interviews. Topical issues are discussed, and programs are usually divided into short segments.

Ideas for... PRESENTING THE LISTENING SKILL: Identifying Important Details

Review the information in the box as a class. Explain that important details not only help listeners understand and remember the main ideas, but can also help them visualize the ideas.

Ideas for... PRESENTING THE NOTE-TAKING SKILL: Using Abbreviations

Ask volunteers to describe how they use abbreviations when they are taking notes. Have students share other useful abbreviations not listed in the box. Write their ideas on the board for reference.

C [1.12] **Note Taking** *(page 27)*

Have students recall any main ideas or details they remember from the radio show before they listen to it again.

AFTER LISTENING

D *(page 27)*

Review note-taking strategies as a class. Have volunteers come up to the board and write down the abbreviations they used in exercise C.

E Critical Thinking: Reflecting *(page 27)*

Ask volunteers to summarize the main points of their discussions for the class.

ANSWER KEY

LISTENING

A *(page 26)*

   1.–2. Answers will vary.

   3. Possible answer: Doctors use computers to review a patient's medical history, to see x-rays, and to prescribe medications.

B *(page 26)* **1.** b; **2.** b; **3.** a

C *(page 27)* Possible answers:

   1. See most pop. + reliable sites / Don't see sites we're not int'ed in

   2. Can do machine lrn'g / Have knowl. of Internet

   3. Can read much info. quickly / Can see things docs don't

E *(page 27)* Answers will vary.

Ideas for... PRESENTING GRAMMAR FOR SPEAKING: Action and Nonaction Verbs

Have students write a "P" by the action verbs that show physical activity and an "M" next to the ones that show mental activity. Ask them to come up with two more examples of action verbs for each category. Then ask them to look at the nonaction verbs and categorize each verb as a state of mind, an emotion, one of the senses, or an indication of possession. Ask them to come up with one more example of a nonaction verb for each category. Review answers and student ideas as a class. Possible answers:

Action Verbs:

1. P: *bring, eat, replace, work, build, run, speak*
2. M: *decide, worry*
3. P or M: *compare, happen, increase, occur, respond*

Nonaction Verbs:

1. State of mind: *be, remember, think, believe, know, matter, understand, mean, seem*
2. Emotion: *love, like, need, prefer, want*
3. One of the senses: *hear, see*
4. Indication of possession: *own, have*

Ideas for... EXPANSION

Write on the board: *What are your family and friends doing right now?* Have students write three sentences with action verbs and three with nonaction verbs to answer the question. If appropriate, encourage students to show photos of their family and friends as they share their answers with a partner.

A *(page 28)*

Explain to students that they should write "C" if the verb form is correct and "I" if it is not. Have students complete the exercise individually and then form pairs to compare answers.

B Personalizing (page 29)

Discuss answers as a class.

> **Ideas for… PRESENTING THE SPEAKING SKILL:**
> **Giving Reasons**
>
> Have students work individually to list reasons for their answers to question 2 in exercise B. On the board, make a T-chart with the title *Young children use smartphones and computers*. Title the left column *Good idea* and the right column *Bad idea*. Ask two volunteers to take notes on the board as you elicit reasons for each side from the class. Then have students debate the topic in pairs. After 5 minutes, tell students to take the other side in the debate. Remind them to use the words and phrases listed in the skill box.

C Personalizing (page 29)

ANSWER KEY

SPEAKING

A *(page 28)* **1.** C; **2.** I (correct form: believe); **3.** C; **4.** C; **5.** I (correct form: do you own); **6.** I (correct form: does not/doesn't matter); **7.** I (correct form: 're/are having); **8.** C

B *(page 29)* Answers will vary.

C *(page 29)* Possible answers:

1. Because I am studying English, I am learning about the culture as well.
2. I am reading a book, since all my friends are using cell phones.
3. I enjoy spending time with my best friend because he likes to do fun activities.
4. Since I'm a social person, I usually go out with my friends on weekends.
5. My family lives in Spain. For this reason, I travel there a couple times a year.

LESSON TASK: DISCUSSING SELF-DRIVING CARS

35 MINS

A Personalizing (page 30)

Read the information in the box together as a class. Clarify any new terms such as *automatic parallel parking* and *lane-assist warnings*. Show examples of each, if necessary.

B Critical Thinking: Evaluating (page 30)

Ask students follow-up questions to increase understanding, such as:

- How might self-driving cars prevent accidents? *(humans get distracted, machines do not)*
- How could self-driving cars communicate and cooperate with each other? *(through GPS systems)*
- How could self-driving cars help people who are unable to drive? *(reduce physical effort needed)*

C Critical Thinking: Interpreting A Bar Graph (page 31)

Review answers as a class.

D Critical Thinking: Reflecting (page 31)

Have volunteers share their opinions with the class.

E Critical Thinking: Analyzing (page 31)

Take a class poll on how many people would ride in a self-driving car. Write the numbers of people who would and wouldn't on the board for reference. Help students calculate percentages, if necessary.

ANSWER KEY

LESSON TASK

A *(page 30)* Answers will vary.

B *(page 30)* Possible answers:

Pros: People could do other things while riding in cars. There would be less of a chance of getting lost.

Cons: The computer in the car might stop working or lose the GPS or Internet connection.

C *(page 31)*

1. How likely people from different countries are to try a self-driving car
2. India has the highest, and Japan has the lowest.
3. Answers will vary.
4. Possible answer: Busy people will likely use self-driving cars, but people who don't trust technology will not.

D–E *(page 31)* Answers will vary.

Video

 VIEWING: *CAN ROBOTS LEARN TO BE MORE HUMAN?* (page 32)

Overview of the Video

National Geographic Explorer, computer scientist, and robotics expert Chad Jenkins explains how coming breakthroughs in robotics will soon make robots a bigger part of everyday life, helping us perform more tasks in our homes and workplaces.

BEFORE VIEWING

A **Critical Thinking: Analyzing** (page 32)

Explain, or ask a volunteer to explain, what a soccer referee does and what a red penalty card means.

B (page 32)

Ask students to predict what they will learn in the video based on the new words and phrases.

TIP Predicting the video content helps students understand it better when they view it.

C **Critical Thinking: Analyzing** (page 33)

Give students a couple minutes to write down one thing they would ask a robot to do. Then call on students individually to share their ideas with the class.

WHILE VIEWING

D ▶ **1.3** **Understanding Details** (page 33)

Give students time to review the statements before they watch the video.

E ▶ **1.3** **Understanding Details** (page 33)

Ask students what questions they still have about robots. See whether anyone in the class can provide answers.

AFTER VIEWING

F **Critical Thinking: Analyzing** (page 33)

Give students a chance to report on their discussions—either by calling on different groups to share their ideas with the class or by having students change groups and tell their new groups about their discussions.

Lesson B

VOCABULARY
30 MINS

A 🎧 **1.13** **Meaning from Context** *(page 34)*

Play the audio two times. The first time, have students listen for the words in blue. The second time, have students listen for the main ideas.

> **Ideas for... CHECKING COMPREHENSION**
>
> Help students summarize the main ideas in the text by asking them to complete these sentences:
> 1. *Germany has a goal of … and it will meet this goal by …*
> 2. *… solves problems for many people in India by …*

B *(page 35)*

As you go over the answers, help students identify the context clues that helped them choose the correct word for each definition.

C **Critical Thinking: Analyzing** *(page 35)*

Explain to students that "IQ" is short for intelligence quotient, a number used to indicate an individual's relative intelligence. As a review, ask students to share how many of their answers were right.

D **Critical Thinking: Evaluating** *(page 35)*

For question 2, ask each group to decide on either individuals or groups. Give them 5 to 10 minutes to discuss this. Have a spokesperson from each group summarize their answer and reasons for the class.

ANSWER KEY

VOCABULARY

B *(page 35)* **1.** alternative; **2.** fossil fuels; **3.** worldwide; **4.** individual; **5.** innovative; **6.** carbon; **7.** cut back on; **8.** impact; **9.** gradual; **10.** consumes

C *(page 35)* Student answers will vary, but the actual answers are shown at the bottom of the page.

D *(page 35)*
1. Possible answer: People could not use heaters or air conditioners and unplug electronics when not in use.
2. Possible answer: I think that companies have a more significant impact on saving energy because they use so much more energy than individual people.
3. Answers will vary.

LISTENING: A CONVERSATION ABOUT TECHNOLOGY
45 MINS

BEFORE LISTENING

A 🎧 **1.14** *(page 36)*

Ask students what they know about Baltimore. Show them where the city is located on a U.S. map. If possible, show a real-life photo of Baltimore's Mr. Trash Wheel as students read and listen to the information.

B **Critical Thinking: Interpreting A Graphic** *(page 36)*

Review answers as a class. Then have students form pairs and explain, step by step, how Mr. Trash Wheel works. Remind them to use transition words such as *first*, *second*, *then*, etc. Ask a volunteer to describe the process aloud for the class.

WHILE LISTENING

C 🎧 **1.15** **Listening for Main Ideas** *(page 37)*

Have students form pairs and compare answers.

D 🎧 **1.15** **Listening for Details** *(page 37)*

Call on volunteers to read sentences that include the correct answer aloud.

AFTER LISTENING

E **Critical Thinking: Synthesizing** *(page 37)*

Tell students to discuss the question in pairs but write their ideas in their charts individually.

F **Critical Thinking: Synthesizing** *(page 37)*

Have a volunteer from each group share which new technology they discussed and how it could be helpful.

> **Ideas for... EXPANSION**
>
> Have students get back in pairs. Explain that each pair will write a short letter, addressed to the Maryland Department of the Environment, proposing their new idea. The letter should clearly explain their idea and provide at least two reasons why it will help Mr. Trash Wheel have a bigger impact on the environment.

LISTENING

B *(page 36)* **1.** b; **2.** d; **3.** e; **4.** a; **5.** c

C *(page 37)*

1. water power and solar power

2. the water wheel

3. A live Internet feed and social media presence adds humor, which makes the public more interested in Mr. Trash Wheel.

D *(page 37)* **1.** city; **2.** 90; **3.** soda; **4.** eyes; **5.** might build

E *(page 37)* The Internet is used to control the speed of the wheel, to reach people on social media, and to reach people via the live stream on the website.

F *(page 37)* Answers will vary.

 SPEAKING

A Critical Thinking: Analyzing *(page 38)*

If possible, show before and after photos of the technology listed in the box to which students can refer as they discuss it.

B Critical Thinking: Evaluating *(page 38)*

Review the modals for advice in the *Everyday Language* box. Explain that *should (not)* and *had better (not)* have a similar meaning but that *had better (not)* may be used to give more urgent advice, which may have bad consequences if it is not followed. Provide additional examples, if necessary.

C Personalizing *(page 39)*

Ask students to brainstorm bad consequences for question 3. Ask "What might happen if your personal information gets stolen online? How can individuals and companies prevent this from happening?"

> **Ideas for... PRESENTING PRONUNCIATION:** Stressed Content Words
>
> 🎧 **1.16** Read the example sentences aloud. Overexaggerate the stressed words. Ask students to repeat them.

D *(page 39)*

Have students form pairs to compare answers and identify the part of speech for each content word.

E 🎧 **1.17** *(page 39)*

Ask volunteers to read the sentences aloud for the class.

SPEAKING

A *(page 38)*

1. Possible answer: Cameras are in phones, computers are getting lighter, and the Internet is more accessible.

2. Possible answer: Mobile phone apps help people spread and receive important information quickly.

3. Answers will vary.

B–C *(page 38)* Answers will vary.

D *(page 39)*

1. <u>Nabila</u> is <u>taking</u> a <u>course</u> in <u>computer programming</u>.

2. <u>Samir wants</u> to <u>become</u> a <u>software designer</u>.

3. <u>All</u> of my <u>friends</u> have <u>cell phones</u>.

4. <u>Large televisions consume</u> a <u>lot</u> of <u>electricity</u>.

5. I'm <u>trying</u> to <u>cut back</u> on the <u>time</u> I <u>spend online</u>.

6. <u>Kenji wants</u> to <u>buy</u> a <u>phone</u> with a <u>better camera</u>.

FINAL TASK: PRESENTING A NEW TECHNOLOGY PRODUCT

A **Brainstorming** *(page 39)*

Have each pair of students share the problems they listed. Write ideas on the board for student reference.

B *(page 39)*

Make sure you approve the topic before students move on. Try to have a variety of topics represented.

C **Brainstorming** *(page 39)*

Encourage students to be creative as they brainstorm. They could create a diagram or a drawing to help them design their new technology product.

D **Organizing Ideas** *(page 40)*

Students may need help conducting research to determine whether their new product already exists. If it does, suggest they design at least one aspect of the product to be different. Give students plenty of time to complete this exercise.

E *(page 40)*

Review and model some co-presenting tips with the class, such as respectful turn taking and standing on different sides of the room. Suggest that partners develop signals such as a head nod for "your turn."

> ### Ideas for... PRESENTING THE PRESENTATION SKILL: Making Eye Contact
>
> It's common for students to present to just the teacher or one or two classmates with whom they are comfortable. Review the information in the box and model effective eye contact, exaggerating the difference between staring and making eye contact. Elicit students' ideas about the benefits of effective eye contact, such as demonstrating presenter confidence and increasing audience interest.

F **Presenting** *(page 40)*

Give students time to reflect on their experience co-presenting—either by journaling or sharing their feedback with their partners. Ask "What do you think you and your partner did well? What would you do differently the next time you co-present?"

ANSWER KEY

FINAL TASK *(pages 39–40)*

A–F Answers will vary.

REFLECTION

- Have students answer questions 1 and 2 on their own, and then discuss their answers in pairs or small groups.
- Ask students to discuss similarities and differences in their answers for questions 1 and 2.
- For question 3, have students compare answers and then write the words about which they are still unsure on the board. Lead a class review of the challenging words and reteach terms as necessary.

3 CULTURE AND TRADITION

UNIT OVERVIEW

In many countries, traditional ways of life are being forgotten as more people leave their homes in rural areas for the city. Some people see this as a sign that their lives are improving, while others regret losing long-held cultural beliefs and customs.

- **LISTENING A A Lecture about Cowboys:** A professor gives a lecture about the traditional cowboy way of life in the United States and Mexico and how it has changed over the years.

- **VIDEO *Faces of India:*** National Geographic Contributing Photographer Steve McCurry has worked all over the world, but for him, nowhere else is as exciting as the remote villages of a large Indian state north of Mumbai on the Pakistan border called Rajasthan. India is one of McCurry's favorite places to photograph because of the richness of the culture.

- **LISTENING B An Assignment about Music:** A professor explains an assignment to the class, and then a student gives a presentation about a type of music from the Roma people of Romania.

For the final task, students draw upon what they have learned in the unit to give an individual presentation about a kind of music that they choose.

For additional information about the topics in this unit, here are some suggestions for online search terms: *cowboys, gift-giving customs, holiday celebrations, wedding traditions, charros, vaqueros, paniolos, gauchos, Holi, Rajasthan India, world music, Roma people, Roma music, Roma culture, bagpipes, Scottish music, Irish music, steel drums, Trinidadian music, Caribbean music*

 **UNIT OPENER** 20 MINS

THINK AND DISCUSS *(page 41)*

Direct students' attention to the photo, title, and caption. Ask leading questions, such as:
- Where is the man in the photo? *(Montana's Judith Basin, USA)*
- How would you describe the weather? *(snowy, cold)*
- How would you describe his clothes? *(cold-weather clothes such as a heavy jacket, scarf, hat)*

ANSWER KEY

THINK AND DISCUSS *(page 41)* Possible answers:
1. He's an American cowboy. He's walking through the snow with his horse.
2. They live off the land and work with cattle and horses.
3. Cowboys live in many countries on different continents including the Americas, Europe, Australia, and Africa.

EXPLORE THE THEME *(pages 42–43)*

Have students describe the photos and read the captions aloud in pairs. Ask students whether they can relate to the photos. Ask "Have you ever been in a similar situation?"

Ideas for… EXPANSION

Have students form pairs or small groups and role-play a gift-giving situation. Give them 5 minutes to brainstorm a traditional event and cultural setting, then 5 minutes to practice before acting out the situation in front of the class. Ask each group to teach the class how to give and receive a gift in the culture presented.

ANSWER KEY

EXPLORE THE THEME *(pages 42–43)*
1. The young woman in the large photo is receiving a gift because it's her 15th birthday. The woman in the photo on the right is receiving gifts because she's going to have a baby. The people are receiving gifts because it's Chinese New Year.
2.–4. Answers will vary.

Lesson A

VOCABULARY
30 MINS

A 🎧 1.18 **Meaning from Context** *(page 44)*

As a review, have volunteers read the completed sentences aloud.

B *(page 44)*

Review answers. Ask students how each word in blue from exercise A is related to the correct word in parentheses. For example, a *custom* is something that people *usually* do.

C 🎧 1.19 *(page 45)*

Work on question 1 together as a class. Read the sentence aloud, ask the class for the answer, and ask what context clues helped them choose that answer. (The words *Western* and *United States* are areas of a country or of the world).

Ideas for… EXPANSION

In small groups, have students research the life and culture of another traditional profession, such as China's lantern makers, or coal miners in Great Britain, and present their findings to the class.

Ideas for… MULTI-LEVEL CLASSES

Arrange students in mixed-level groups for the expansion activity. Assign roles so that all group members participate. Lower-level students can be researchers while higher-level students can be recorders, taking notes and writing up the research, and reporters, using the recorders' text to report back to the whole class. Tell them to use the text in exercise C as a model. Encourage them to write two paragraphs if possible.

D **Personalizing** *(page 45)*

Allow time for students to complete the sentences individually first.

Ideas for… EXPANSION

Write different aspects of culture on the board, such as: *history, art, social groups, economy, medicine, daily life, government, food, clothes*. Review the terms with the class for meaning. Ask students to write down three additional questions they have about their partner's cultural traditions in one or more of these areas. Give students time to write their sentences, then have them continue the conversation in the same pairs when ready.

ANSWER KEY

VOCABULARY

A *(page 44)* **1.** usually; **2.** more; **3.** reason for; **4.** haven't; **5.** long; **6.** making plans; **7.** no one; **8.** areas; **9.** keep; **10.** don't know

B *(page 44)* **1.** a; **2.** f; **3.** e; **4.** c; **5.** j; **6.** h; **7.** i; **8.** b; **9.** d; **10.** g

C *(page 45)* **1.** region; **2.** factor; **3.** estimate; **4.** developed; **5.** customs; **6.** traditional; **7.** still; **8.** disappeared; **9.** actual; **10.** preserve

D *(page 45)* Answers will vary.

LISTENING: A LECTURE ABOUT COWBOYS

BEFORE LISTENING

A **Prior Knowledge** *(page 46)*

Encourage students to use the new vocabulary words as they discuss the questions.

WHILE LISTENING

Ideas for... EXPANSION

Have students analyze the two portraits on page 46 in pairs. Ask them to have a discussion based on the following questions:

1. How are these images different from other images in this unit?
2. How do you think these men are feeling? Why?
3. Do the photos help you understand anything else about cowboys? If so, what?

B 🎧 1.20 ▶ 1.4 **Listening for Main Ideas** *(page 46)*

Read through the two questions and possible answers as a class. Tell students to listen for the main ideas.

C 🎧 1.20 **Listening for Details** *(page 47)*

Read the notes and discuss what kind of information is missing before listening to the lecture again.

D 🎧 1.20 **Critical Thinking: Making Inferences** *(page 47)*

Give students time to read through the statements before listening to the lecture again.

E *(page 47)*

When you are going over the answers, make sure students explain the evidence in the lecture on which they based their answer choices.

AFTER LISTENING

Ideas for... CHECKING COMPREHENSION

Ask students to come up with a list of typical characteristics that represent a cowboy's way of life based on the information in the lecture. Have a volunteer write the list on the board. Encourage students to refer to this list while they are completing exercise F.

F **Critical Thinking: Reflecting** *(page 47)*

Take a class poll to see how many students would like the cowboy way of life.

TIP Having students make generalizations about a text, audio, or video is a powerful critical thinking exercise, but be sure they know the difference between valid (true) and faulty (false) generalizations. A valid generalization is supported by facts, is based on logic and reasoning, and is proven with several examples. A faulty generalization is not supported by facts. Teach students key words that are often used to make faulty generalizations, such as *none*, *all*, *always*, *never*, *everyone*, and *nobody*. Suggest better alternatives such as *most of the time* or *many people*.

ANSWER KEY

LISTENING

A *(page 46)* Answers will vary.

B *(page 46)*
1. b. The United States; c. Mexico
2. a. photos; c. information about modern cowboys

C *(page 47)*
Tyrel Tucker: 2 years old, 2,300, electricity
Manuel Rodriguez: 4 years old, married, move back

D *(page 47)*
1. F (He didn't like to be indoors.)
2. F (They ate the same three foods. A healthy diet includes a variety of foods.)
3. T (Tyrel loves the outdoors, and Manuel plans to move back to the countryside.)
4. F (They both like working as cowboys, and they never mention wanting a different job.)

E *(page 47)* Answers will vary.

F *(page 47)*
1. Answers will vary.
2. Possible answer: He probably used an old camera to give the images a more traditional look.
3. Possible answer: Some people might still want to be cowboys today because it gives them a lot of freedom and allows them to be in nature.
4. Answers will vary.

SPEAKING

Ideas for... PRESENTING THE SPEAKING SKILL:
Asking for and Giving Clarification

Ask students how comfortable they are asking for or giving clarification and why. Model the rising and falling intonation of each expression. Give students time to practice the expressions aloud in pairs.

A 🎧 **1.21** *(pages 48–49)*

Play the audio two times. The first time, tell students to listen for the missing phrases. The second time, tell them to listen for main ideas and important details.

Ideas for... EXPANSION

Arrange students in groups of three. Have them decide who will role-play Emily, Professor Diaz, and Liam. Ask them to practice the conversation several times to increase fluency. Remind them to pay attention to their intonation when asking for and giving clarification. Invite volunteers to role-play the conversation in front of the class.

B **Asking for and Giving Clarification** *(page 49)*

Call on several pairs of students to present one of their short conversations for the class.

Ideas for... EXPANSION

Ask students to choose a topic related to the theme of this unit. Invite three or four volunteers to form a panel of experts on this topic. Ask them to sit at the front of the class. They will give a talk about one aspect of the topic while members of the "audience" interrupt them to ask for clarification.

Ideas for... PRESENTING GRAMMAR FOR
SPEAKING: The Past Continuous

Have students take turns asking and answering questions about what they were doing at specific times in the past. For example:

A: What were you doing at 6 p.m. yesterday?

B: I was doing my homework.

C **Critical Thinking: Analyzing** *(page 49)*

Ask for volunteers to explain why each sentence uses the past continuous.

D *(page 50)*

Have students underline the time expression in each question as they complete the exercise.

E **Personalizing** *(page 50)*

Remind students that follow-up questions are more effective when they are open-ended *wh-* questions.

F **Critical Thinking: Reflecting** *(page 50)*

Have students talk to a different classmate for each question. Keep time, and give each pair of students 5 minutes to share their stories for each question before they find new partners.

Ideas for... EXPANSION

Have students do a mingle activity. Ask them to write three questions using the past continuous to get to know their classmates better. They can be more general questions about culture, such as Why were the politicians arguing over health care last week?, or they can be specific questions about the person's daily routine, such as Where were you going after class yesterday? Give them time to write the questions then ask them to stand up and ask their questions to at least three different classmates. Encourage them to ask follow-up questions to keep the conversation going.

ANSWER KEY

SPEAKING

A *(pages 48–49)*

1. Could you please explain
2. Could you explain
3. I'm afraid I still don't understand
4. put it another way
5. do you mean that
6. I said that

B *(page 49)* Answers will vary.

C *(page 49)*

1. was ...running (reason #2)
2. was working (reason #1)
3. was singing, was making (reason #3)

D *(page 50)* **1.** was studying; **2.** was living; **3.** was cleaning, were watching; **4.** was doing; **5.** was driving; **6.** wasn't/was not raining; **7.** were talking, was giving; **8.** were, laughing

E–F *(page 50)* Answers will vary.

LESSON TASK: EXCHANGING INFORMATION ABOUT COWBOYS

 A *(page 50)*

Have students form pairs and decide who is student A and who is student B. Ask them to read their paragraph individually first and then answer the questions with a classmate who read the same paragraph.

TIP Encourage students to annotate text as they read by underlining main ideas; circling unfamiliar vocabulary; and signaling important information with notes, key words, or symbols in the margin.

B *(page 51)*

Have students return to their original partner and summarize the main points in their paragraph. Ask them to repeat the activity several times to increase fluency.

> Ideas for... **EXPANSION**
>
> Ask students "What about this information surprises you? Would you like to live one of these lifestyles? Why or why not?" Encourage them to give reasons and specific examples for their opinions as they discuss these questions in pairs.

> Ideas for... **MULTI-LEVEL CLASSES**
>
> To make exercise B more challenging, higher-level students should report on their paragraph without using their notes.

 ANSWER KEY

LESSON TASK

A and B *(pages 50–51)*

Student A, *Paniolos*

1. It's about traditional Hawaiian cowboys called *paniolos*. They live in Hawaii.

2. They controlled the cattle and taught cattle-handling skills to the local people. They were Mexican men living in California before they moved to the island.

3. Now, there are only a few large ranches and a few old paniolos left.

Student B, *Gauchos*

1. It's about cowboys of Brazil, Argentina, and Uruguay called *gauchos*.

2. They worked on different farms but were very poor. People admired them for their independence, bravery, and horseback riding skills.

3. Now most of them receive a steady salary and work only in one place.

 # Video

 **VIEWING:** *FACES OF INDIA* *(page 52)*

Overview of the Video

National Geographic Contributing Photographer Steve McCurry has worked all over the world, but for him, nowhere else is as exciting as the remote villages of a large Indian state north of Mumbai on the Pakistan border called Rajasthan. India is one of McCurry's favorite places to photograph because of the richness of the culture.

BEFORE VIEWING

A **Meaning from Context** *(page 52)*

Ask students what they know about India and Rajasthan. Review the pronunciation of the words Rajasthan (**rah**-juh-stahn) and Rajasthani (rah-juh-**stah**-nee) with the class. Have students take turns reading the sections of the text aloud in pairs.

> Ideas for... **CHECKING COMPREHENSION**
>
> Write on the board: Occupations, Clothing, Music and Dance, Way of Life, and People. Give students one minute to individually review the information in exercise A. When time is up, ask them to cover the text and take turns giving details to a partner about the Rajasthani people according to the five topics listed on the board. Keep track of time, and give each partner two minutes to speak. Repeat the exercise as many times as possible to increase fluency.

B *(page 53)*

Have students work with the same partners they had for exercise A.

C **Personalizing** *(page 53)*

Have volunteers share what visitors from other countries appreciate about their culture with the class.

> Ideas for... **EXPANSION**
>
> After reading the information about Steve McCurry, ask students to reflect on the benefits and challenges of living in a new culture. Ask: What are the benefits of living in a new culture? What is difficult about living in a culture that is very different from your own? Would you want Steve McCurry's job? Why or why not? Encourage them to use examples from their own experience as they discuss the questions in small groups.

WHILE VIEWING

D ▶ 1.5 **Understanding Main Ideas** *(page 53)*

Give students time to read the statements and guess whether each is true or false. As you go over the answers, ask students how they changed the false statements to make them true.

E ▶ 1.5 **Understanding Details** *(page 53)*

Have students explain why each answer is an example of traditional culture.

AFTER VIEWING

F **Critical Thinking: Analyzing** *(page 53)*

Encourage students to continue the conversation by sharing whether they would like the Rajasthani lifestyle.

ANSWER KEY

VIDEO

B *(page 53)* **1.** nomads; **2.** shepherds; **3.** careers; **4.** hospitable; **5.** landscape; **6.** entertainers

D *(page 53)* **1.** F (He worked for a newspaper.); **2.** F (It's on the border of Pakistan.); **3.** T; **4.** T; **5.** F (It takes him some time.)

E *(page 53)*
- ✓ moving animals from place to place
- ✓ entertainers working with snakes
- ✓ traditional clothing
- ✓ traditional houses

F *(page 53)* Answers will vary.

Lesson B

⏱ 30 MINS **VOCABULARY**

A 🎧 1.22 **Meaning from Context** *(page 54)*

Before they listening to the assignment, ask students why music is important to culture and what can be expressed through music.

B *(page 54)*

Point out that the words are all nouns or verbs and that this can be a clue to matching them with their definitions.

> **Ideas for… CHECKING COMPREHENSION**
>
> Write the following words on the board, and ask students to use them to summarize the assignment in exercise A: *select, describe, explain, compare, define, summarize.*

> **Ideas for… PRESENTING THE VOCABULARY SKILL:** Keeping A Vocabulary Journal
>
> Have students choose two more words from exercise B and write two vocabulary journal entries following the model in the skill box.

C **Personalizing** *(page 55)*

Have students repeat the exercise as a mingling activity to increase fluency. Ask them to stand up and talk to a different classmate for each question as you keep track of the time.

ANSWER KEY

VOCABULARY

B *(page 54)* **1.** e; **2.** j; **3.** g; **4.** d; **5.** b; **6.** c; **7.** f; **8.** a; **9.** h; **10.** i

C *(page 55)* Answers will vary.

LISTENING: AN ASSIGNMENT ABOUT MUSIC

BEFORE LISTENING

A Prior Knowledge *(page 56)*

Ask students for other examples of people who live in many different countries but have kept their own culture and language.

WHILE LISTENING

> **Ideas for... PRESENTING THE NOTE-TAKING SKILL:**
> Using A Numbered List
>
> Ask students whether they like to organize their notes with a numbered list. Have them share why or why not.

B 🎧 1.23 Note Taking *(page 57)*

Allow time for students to read the notes and think about what information is missing. Ask them what key words they should listen for, such as *talk about, aspects, compare, summarize,* etc.

> **Ideas for... EXPANSION**
>
> Ask students to think of something they know how to do really well. Give examples such as make pasta, install a new software, or play a favorite video game. Individually, have them take notes on a step-by-step explanation of how to complete this activity using a numbered list. Each step should have just one piece of information. Then, have students take turns sharing their explanations in pairs. Partner A states his or her skill and explains how to complete the activity. Remind partner A not to show his or her notes to partner B. As partner A speaks, partner B should take notes in a numbered list. When finished, students can compare their notes. Students should repeat this activity for partner B.

> **Ideas for... PRESENTING THE LISTENING SKILL:**
> Asking Questions While Listening
>
> Remind students that it will take practice to develop this habit. Provide them with additional examples of *yes/no* or *wh-* questions they can ask while listening. For example:
> 1. *How does this relate to what was said before?*
> 2. *How does this relate to what I already know?*
> 3. *What's the point he's trying to make?*
> 4. *How is that helpful? How can I use this?*
> 5. *Does this make sense?*
> 6. *Do I understand what she's saying or should I ask for clarification?*

C 🎧 1.24 Listening for Main Ideas *(page 57)*

Remind students to circle the numbers of the parts of the assignment in exercise B as each student says them in his or her presentation. Play the audio again, if necessary.

AFTER LISTENING

D *(page 57)*

Review the answers as a class. Ask students to evaluate the presentation. What did they like about it? What do they think could be improved?

E Personalizing *(page 57)*

If possible, play a sample of Roma music by the Shukar Collective for the class. Ask "Is it what you expected? Do you like this style of music? Why or why not?"

ANSWER KEY
LISTENING
A *(page 56)* Answers will vary.
B *(page 57)*
1. select, music, culture
2. culture
3. describe, explain, traditional, modern
4. contrast, music
5. play
6. main, questions
C *(page 57)* He includes 1, 2, 3, and 6; he doesn't include 4 and 5.
E *(page 57)* Answers will vary.

A Personalizing *(page 58)*

Review the names and pronunciations of a variety of musical instruments. If possible, show images as well.

B *(page 58)*

Have students form pairs and decide who is student A and who is student B. Ask them to read their paragraph individually first and then answer the questions with a classmate who read the same paragraph.

C *(page 59)*

Have students return to their original partner and summarize the main points in their paragraph. Ask them to repeat the activity several times to increase fluency.

Ideas for… PRESENTING PRONUNCIATION: Reduced Function Words

🎧 **1.25** Explain that *reduced forms* are words that are not stressed and are often joined. These forms are sometimes represented as a contraction, a shortened version of the written and spoken word created by leaving out some letters and sounds. Other times, these forms are not formally represented, only heard. Play the audio and have students repeat the reduced function words several times.

D 🎧 1.26 *(page 59)*

Before listening to the audio, ask students to explain how they identified the function words in each sentence. Note that the verb *be* is not technically a function word (auxiliary) in the chart and in sentence 1, but it is often contracted and reduced.

E *(page 59)*

Have volunteers say the sentences aloud for the class.

Ideas for… EXPANSION

Have students look back at the texts about paniolos and gauchos in exercise A on page 51. Ask them to work in pairs to choose and analyze six sentences from these texts. First, have them write down any six sentences from the two texts on a separate piece of paper. Then, have them underline the function words in those sentences. Finally, ask them to take turns saying the sentences aloud. Remind them to reduce the function words. Have volunteers say their sentences aloud for the class.

SPEAKING

A *(page 58)* Answers will vary.

B *(page 58)*

Student A, *Bagpipes*

1. Bagpipes are an old instrument. They have a large bag that holds air and one or more small pipes that make the notes of the music. They are most famously played in Scotland and Ireland.
2. The player blows air into the bag, and the air comes out slowly through the pipes.
3. Bagpipes have a long history.

Student B, *Steel Drums*

1. Steel drums are made from old steel oil barrels. They are from Trinidad.
2. The top of the drum has different sections, and each section makes a different musical note.
3. Steel drums are relatively new, and they sound light and happy. They are a popular instrument at the *Carnival* festival in Trinidad every year.

D *(page 59)*

1. The violin is my favorite instrument.
2. Our friends are waiting outside.
3. Only a few people play this kind of guitar.
4. You can probably hear it on the radio.
5. The group is playing in a small theater.
6. Tell Maria about the class assignment.

FINAL TASK: PRESENTING A KIND OF MUSIC

A Brainstorming (page 60)

This exercise can be done in small groups or as a class. Play short samples of different types of music (e.g., jazz, reggae, opera), and ask students to identify the genre. Invite students to come up to the board and write the name of a genre with which they are familiar or like. Leave the results of the brainstorming session on the board for reference.

B Organizing Ideas (page 60)

Make sure you approve the students' presentation topics before they move on to question 2. Suggest that students take notes on a separate piece of paper or notecards.

TIP It will be more interesting for the class if each student chooses a different type of music for his or her presentation. You can facilitate this by asking students to write down a first, second, and third choice to use for their presentations. Make note of which topics are already taken before you approve each student's topic.

> ### Ideas for… PRESENTING THE PRESENTATION
> ### SKILL: Using Good Posture
>
> Read the information in the box. Explain that good posture helps to convey confidence and makes a presentation clearer. For example, if you stand up straight and look directly at your audience (not at your notes or at the board), your voice will be clearer and easier to follow. Have volunteers act out examples of good and bad posture for giving presentations.

C Presenting (page 60)

Before presentations start, clarify the criteria for evaluating a presentation. These criteria could include clear organization, eye contact with audience, and good posture. Students can use the criteria to evaluate each other's presentations. Encourage students to raise their hands and ask clarification questions during the talk.

ANSWER KEY

FINAL TASK

A–C (page 60) Answers will vary.

REFLECTION

- Have students answer questions 1 and 2 on their own, and then discuss their answers in pairs or small groups.
- Ask students to discuss similarities and differences in their answers for questions 1 and 2.
- For question 3, have students compare answers and then write the words about which they are still unsure on the board. Lead a class review of the challenging words, and reteach terms as necessary.

A THIRSTY WORLD

4

UNIT OVERVIEW

The theme of this unit is a topic that is essential for our lives—water. In many places around the world, there are extremes of drought or flooding, and not having clean water is a huge problem.

- **LISTENING A A Talk about the Itaipu Dam:** A guest speaker gives a talk about the benefits and problems caused by Brazil and Paraguay's Itaipu Dam.

- **VIDEO *Dam-Release Rafting:*** Dams don't always hold water back; sometimes they have to let it through. A number of thrill seekers who enjoy extreme water sports are requesting the release of water so they can enjoy a day of unconventional white-water rafting in the UK, where the lack of mountains means limited opportunities for whitewater rafting.

- **LISTENING B A Discussion about the Ogallala Aquifer:** A study group has a discussion about the problems faced by people who depend on water from the Ogallala Aquifer and some possible solutions.

For the final task, students draw upon what they have learned in the unit to role-play a government meeting about how to manage the local water supply.

For additional information about the topics in this unit, here are some suggestions for online search terms: *virtual water, irrigation, the Amazon River, the Nile River, renewable resources, Itaipu Dam, Paraná River, hydroelectric power, rainwater collection, conservation, Q Drum, Kickstart Pump, LifeStraw, dam-release rafting, water-stressed areas, Ogallala Aquifer, ways to save water*

 **UNIT OPENER**

THINK AND DISCUSS *(page 61)*

Direct students' attention to the photo, title, and caption. Ask leading questions, such as:

- Who are the people in this photo? *(a man and a woman; could be conservationists)*
- Where are they? *(Ivanhoe Reservoir in Los Angeles California, USA)*

ANSWER KEY

THINK AND DISCUSS *(page 61)*

1. Possible answer: Maybe they are checking on the plastic balls to be sure they are all working properly.

2. Answers will vary, but the student should infer that not enough water (for drinking) is the bigger problem.

EXPLORE THE THEME *(pages 62–63)*

Have students form small groups and take turns reading aloud the different passages and captions. Give them plenty of time to explore the infographic and discuss questions. Walk around the classroom, and offer help and advice as needed.

> **Ideas for... EXPANSION**
>
> Have two volunteers lead a class discussion of the questions and elicit personal experiences from the students. For example, they could ask "Which of these items do you use or consume? How much water do you think you use every day?"

ANSWER KEY

EXPLORE THE THEME *(pages 62–63)*

1. Possible answer: the amount of water needed to produce products; water we consume that we don't see

2. a cup of tea = 9 gallons; a pair of jeans = 2,900 gallons; a T-shirt = 766 gallons; a pound of figs = 379 gallons

3. A diet that includes meat requires more water because of the water required to raise the cattle.

4. Answers will vary.

Lesson A

30 MINS **VOCABULARY**

A 🎧 **1.27** **Meaning from Context** *(page 64)*

After they have listened to the statements, give students time to discuss the meanings of the words in blue in pairs.

B *(page 64)*

Remind students to use context clues to match each word with its definition. Encourage them to use a dictionary, if necessary.

> **Ideas for… EXPANSION**
>
> Ask students to choose four of the vocabulary words and write sentences with the words that are true for them. If applicable, they can include the example sentences in their vocabulary journal entries.

C *(page 65)*

Have students take the quiz individually.

D *(page 65)*

Follow up with a class discussion. Ask "How many answers did you get right? Which numbers did you get wrong? Which statements were the most surprising or shocking? Why?"

TIP When possible, ask a volunteer to lead class discussions.

> **Ideas for… PRESENTING THE VOCABULARY SKILL:** Recognizing Suffixes
>
> Review the verbs and nouns in the table. Ask students to identify the suffix in each example and guess its meaning. (Both *-tion* and *-ment* are used to form nouns meaning "the action of a verb" or "the result of a verb.") Have students point out the suffix in other common words such as *digital*, *educational*, and *environmental*. Ask "How do you think this suffix changes the part of speech or grammatical function of these three words?"

E *(page 65)*

As you review the answers, ask students to point out the suffixes of the words in parentheses.

F **Critical Thinking: Analyzing** *(page 65)*

Encourage students to use vocabulary introduced in this lesson as they discuss the questions. Ask a volunteer from each group to share their group's ideas with the class.

ANSWER KEY

VOCABULARY

B *(page 64)* **1.** g; **2.** h; **3.** c; **4.** i; **5.** j; **6.** d; **7.** f; **8.** a; **9.** e; **10.** b

C–D *(page 65)* **1.** T; **2.** T; **3.** F (About 6 to 8 million people die each year from drinking dirty water.); **4.** F (Around 70% of fresh water is used for farming.); **5.** T; **6.** T; **7.** T; **8.** T; **9.** F (The Nile River flows through 11 different countries.); **10.** F (People in Mozambique in Africa use the smallest amount of water.)

E *(page 65)* **1.** requirement; **2.** collection; **3.** occur; **4.** depend; **5.** management; **6.** require

F *(page 65)*

1. Possible answer: Not enough water can cause dehydration and too much water can cause floods. Many places on the eastern coast of the US have experienced flooding, especially during large storms or hurricanes. The western coast of the US has experienced a lack of water.

2. Possible answer: food, clean air to breathe, a safe place to sleep

3. Answers will vary.

4. Possible answer: Air needs to be clean and forests need to be protected.

LISTENING: A TALK ABOUT THE ITAIPU DAM

45 MINS

BEFORE LISTENING

A Prior Knowledge *(page 66)*

Direct students' attention to the photo, and have them describe what they see. Ask students how this photo might be related to the unit theme.

WHILE LISTENING

B 🎧 1.28 ▶ 1.6 Listening for Main Ideas *(page 66)*

After they have listened to the talk, have students discuss in pairs why they think this is the main idea.

> **Ideas for… PRESENTING THE NOTE-TAKING SKILL: Using a T-Chart**
>
> Review the information in the box. Brainstorm the benefits of a T-chart as a class; for example, it's easy to compare and contrast information because it's clearly listed side by side. Have students come up with real-life situations in which they might want to use a T-chart, such as for comparing issues related to politics, choosing the best health care plan, or making other important life decisions.

C 🎧 1.28 Note Taking *(page 67)*

Give students time to read through the T-chart before listening to the talk again so they know what details to listen for.

AFTER LISTENING

D Critical Thinking: Analyzing *(page 67)*

Have students share which person (or people) with whom they most identify and why.

 **SPEAKING**

> **Ideas for… PRESENTING GRAMMAR FOR SPEAKING: Active and Passive Voice**
>
> Review the information in the box. Call out some regular and irregular verbs, and ask students to tell you the past participle. If necessary, provide students with a list of irregular past participles for reference. Explain to students that the passive voice is also used to be vague about who is responsible ("Mistakes were made.") or to talk about a general truth ("Rules are made to be broken.").

A *(page 68)*

Have students form pairs and compare answers.

B *(page 68)*

Tell students to ask follow-up questions to learn more about their partners. Remind them that follow-up questions should be open-ended *wh-* questions but still be as specific as possible.

> **Ideas for… EXPANSION**
>
> Have students rewrite their sentences from exercise A in the active voice.

C *(page 68)*

Have students change partners so they work with a different classmate. Remind them to use *by* plus the agent in their answers as appropriate. Invite volunteers to write their answers on the board.

> **Ideas for… PRESENTING PRONUNCIATION: Suffixes and Syllable Stress**
>
> 🎧 1.29 Have students count the syllables in the examples and identify which one is stressed in each word. Ask them to describe the difference between the position of the stressed syllable in each example. (It starts as the first or second syllable and then moves to the second, third, or fourth syllable when the suffix is added.) Read the examples aloud, and exaggerate the stressed syllable.

D 🎧 1.30 *(page 69)*

Suggest that students circle the suffix in each word to help them identify the stressed syllable.

E *(page 69)*

Remind students the stressed syllable is usually pronounced a little louder and more clearly than the other syllables.

F Personalizing *(page 69)*

Have students identify the two words in each question that are similar and underline the syllable with the main stress in each. (1. active, activities; 2. define, definition; 3. influence, influential; 4. electricity, electrical)

ANSWER KEY

SPEAKING

A *(page 68)*

1. Rice <u>is grown</u> in countries such as _____. (P, passive)
2. In my country, a lot of electricity <u>is provided</u> by _____. (P, passive)
3. Nowadays, many people <u>study</u> online instead of in _____. (A, active)
4. At my house, we <u>use</u> a significant amount of water for _____. (A, active)
5. In my country, children <u>are taught</u> to _____. (P, passive)
6. My favorite dish <u>is made</u> with _____. (P, passive)

B *(page 68)* Possible answers:

1. Rice is grown in countries such as <u>China and Vietnam</u>.
2. In my country, a lot of electricity is provided by <u>nuclear power plants</u>.
3. Nowadays, many people study online instead of in <u>classrooms</u>.
4. At my house, we use a significant amount of water for <u>taking showers</u>.
5. In my country, children are taught to <u>respect older people</u>.
6. My favorite dish is made with <u>rice and beans</u>.

C *(page 68)* Possible answers:

1. Coffee is grown in Brazil, Colombia, and Indonesia.
2. The apartment next to mine is owned by a couple from Germany.
3. The money in my household is managed by my wife.
4. Smartphones are used for taking photos and sending texts.
5. Coins are collected by people who are interested in history and other cultures.
6. The homework in this class is corrected by our teacher.

D *(page 69)*

1. **po**litics — It was a significant po**li**tical event.
2. **re**sident — This is a resi**den**tial apartment building.
3. ap**ply** — We turned in our appli**ca**tion before the due date.
4. **po**ssible — There is a possi**bil**ity of finding water on other planets.
5. in**form** — We need more infor**ma**tion before we make a decision.
6. **theo**ry — This is only a theo**re**tical situation. It's not real.

F *(page 69)* Answers will vary.

LESSON TASK: PRESENTING A CLEAN WATER DEVICE

35 MINS

A **Critical Thinking: Evaluating** *(pages 70–71)*

Put students into groups of three. Read the situation, and explain that each group will choose one of the three devices to present. Give groups 5 minutes to read and discuss the questions for the first device. Then review the answers as a class before they move on to the next one. Repeat for each device.

B **Organizing Ideas** *(page 71)*

Walk around, and monitor group work. Help students express their ideas in the passive voice when needed.

> **Ideas for… PRESENTING THE PRESENTATION SKILL: Speaking at the Right Volume**
>
> Remind students that the "right" volume will depend on where they are presenting. Elicit examples of different contexts that might require a lower volume (meeting room) or a higher volume (lecture hall).

C **Presenting** *(page 71)*

When all the presentations have been completed, have the class vote on which clean water device is best.

LESSON TASK

A *(pages 70-71)* Possible sentences about the devices:

Device 1 The Q Drum

The drum is used to bring clean water to houses.

A rope is put through a hole in the drum.

The drum is pulled, not carried.

The drums are made in South Africa.

The drums are sold for $70.

Device 2 The KickStart Pump

The pump is sold to farmers in Africa.

The pump is operated with their feet.

More crops are grown with the water.

The money from the crops is used for the family's health and education.

The pumps are made in Kenya and are sold for $70.

Device 3 The LifeStraw

The LifeStraw can be used with any kind of dirty water.

One end of the straw is put in a person's mouth, and the other end is put into the water.

The LifeStraw is often used in emergency situations and for camping.

No electrical power is required to use the LifeStraw.

The LifeStraw is made by a Swiss company and is sold for $20.

Possible answers to questions on page 70:

1. The drum is used to bring clean water to houses. The pump helps farmers grow more crops. The LifeStraw can clean any kind of dirty water.

2. The Q Drum helps families, the KickStart Pump helps farmers, and the LifeStraw helps individuals.

3. All seem easy to make. The Q Drum and the KickStart Pump are made in Africa, so could probably be transported within Africa easily, but given their size, might be difficult to send to other continents. The LifeStraw is very small and lightweight, so would likely be easy to send globally.

B *(page 71)* Answers will vary.

Video

45 MINS **VIEWING:** *DAM-RELEASE RAFTING* *(page 72)*

Overview of The Video

Dams don't always hold water back; sometimes they have to let it through. A number of thrill seekers who enjoy extreme water sports are requesting the release of water so they can enjoy a day of unconventional white-water rafting in the UK, where the lack of mountains means limited opportunities for whitewater rafting.

BEFORE VIEWING

A *(page 72)*

Read the information in the box aloud. Ask students what other dangerous and exciting activities they know of or have done.

B **Predicting** *(page 72)*

Tell students to use the photo, the video title, and the information in the box to brainstorm ideas for what the video could be about. Explain how predicting helps them integrate new information (what they are going to watch) with information they already know.

WHILE VIEWING

C ▶ **1.7** **Check Predictions** *(page 73)*

Play the video and ask students to circle any words from the previous exercise that they hear.

D ▶ **1.7** **Understanding Details** *(page 73)*

If necessary, pause the video after each quote to give students time to record their answers.

AFTER VIEWING

E *(page 73)*

Have volunteers read the steps aloud to review answers as a class.

F *(page 73)*

Have students switch partners and complete the exercise again to increase fluency.

G Critical Thinking: Analyzing *(page 73)*

Explain to students that the word *risky* describes something involving the possibility of something bad or unpleasant happening, such as an injury or a loss. Ask "Do you enjoy risky activities? Why or why not?"

ANSWER KEY

VIDEO

B *(page 72)* Answers will vary.

C *(page 73)* These items are discussed in the video.

✓ a dam

✓ a raft

✓ a river or stream

✓ how water is released from a dam

D *(page 73)* **1.** 8,000; **2.** 1,500; **3.** 900; **4.** 50; **5.** 10

E *(page 73)* **1.** is requested; **2.** is paid; **3.** is opened; **4.** are carried; **5.** is closed

G *(page 73)* Answers will vary.

Lesson B

VOCABULARY   30 MINS

A Personalizing *(page 74)*

Have volunteers share their personal experiences with water shortages. Ask students how they think water affects our lives.

B 🎧 1.31 Meaning from Context *(page 74)*

After students have listened to the information, ask them to suggest alternative words for the words in blue.

Ideas for... EXPANSION

Have students discuss their first reactions to the listening exercise in groups. Ask "Are you surprised by the information shown on the map? Why or why not? Why do you think large areas in South America, Africa, Asia, and Australia are not 'water stressed'?"

C *(page 75)*

Tell students to look back at the text in exercise B for context clues. Encourage students to use a dictionary to look up the meanings of the words in blue, if necessary.

D Personalizing *(page 75)*

Brainstorm nonverbal ways people can show interest as well. Ask students to use both verbal and nonverbal communication strategies as they discuss the topics.

E Critical Thinking: Interpreting A Map *(page 75)*

Have students find another pair and form a group of four. Ask them to compare answers and share opinions and experiences about question 4.

Ideas for... EXPANSION

Ask students to identify ways that people waste water in their country and make a list of five tips for how to conserve it.

VOCABULARY

A *(page 74)* Answers will vary.

C *(page 75)* **1.** distributed; **2.** conservation; **3.** average; **4.** agriculture; **5.** urgent; **6.** crisis; **7.** reduce; **8.** experienced; **9.** extremely; **10.** scarce

D *(page 75)* Answers will vary.

E *(page 75)*

1. Possible answers: Barcelona, Mumbai, Las Vegas

2. Possible answers: Ghana, Buenos Aires, Guatemala

3. Possible answers: Johannesburg, Kathmandu

4. Answers will vary.

LISTENING: A DISCUSSION ABOUT THE OGALLALA AQUIFER

BEFORE LISTENING

 A *(page 76)*

Review any terms that might be unfamiliar to students, such as *irrigate* (to supply something, such as land, with water by using artificial means) or *pump up* (to move something—such as water, air, or gas—to or from a particular place with a pump).

WHILE LISTENING

B 🎧 **1.32** **Listening for Main Ideas** *(page 76)*

Review answers as a class. Ask students to give reasons for their choices.

> **Ideas for… PRESENTING THE LISTENING SKILL: Listening for Problems and Solutions**
>
> Remind students that a synonym is a word or phrase that means exactly or nearly the same as another word or phrase. Point out that *issue* is a synonym for *problem* and *approach* is a synonym for *solution*. Elicit other synonyms for the words *problem* and *solution* from the class, and write them on the board. Other possible synonyms for *problem* are *complication*, *difficult situation*, *obstacle*, *trouble*, and *worry*. Other possible synonyms for *solution* are *answer*, *response* and *resolution*.

C 🎧 **1.32** **Listening for Problems and Solutions** *(page 77)*

Give students time to review the T-chart before listening to the discussion again.

AFTER LISTENING

D **Critical Thinking: Evaluating** *(page 77)*

Discuss solutions with the class. Have two volunteers debate which solution would have more of an impact.

LISTENING

A *(page 76)*

1. Possible answer: An aquifer is a place underground that contains a lot of water.

2. Possible answer: They use the water to irrigate their fields and grow crops.

3. Possible answer: Because without the water the land would be too dry to grow certain crops.

4. Answers will vary.

B *(page 76)*

1. c. How to Solve the Aquifer Crisis

2. b. people are using the aquifer water too quickly

3. a. it requires little water

C *(page 77)* Possible answers:

The Ogallala Aquifer	
Problems:	Possible Solutions:
- *Water in aquifers being pumped out quickly (past 70 yrs.)* - *In parts of the western U.S., not enough water for 1. people's homes/ drinking or washing* *2. growing food (for crops)*	- *Better ways to distribute water* - *Water conservation, e.g., dryland farming*

D *(page 77)*

1. Answers will vary.

2. Possible answer: People could use less water in their homes.

3. Answers will vary.

> **Ideas for... PRESENTING THE SPEAKING SKILL:**
> Asking for and Giving Opinions
>
> Read through the examples in the box. Have students complete the expressions in their own words.

A **Asking For And Giving Opinions** *(page 78)*

Consider doing this exercise as a mingling activity to prepare students for small-talk situations. Have students walk around and discuss topics. Tell students they should talk to every classmate at least once.

B **Critical Thinking: Applying** *(pages 78–79)*

Have students look at the images and estimate how many times each activity is carried out in a week. Ask them to calculate the total water usage of an average household. Share ideas as a class.

C **Critical Thinking: Prioritizing** *(page 79)*

Have students look at the images in exercise B and decide which of these activities uses the most water and which uses the least. They should use this information to help them list their family's water priorities.

D **Presenting** *(page 79)*

Encourage students to use a visual to help them organize and communicate their ideas. Remind them to use expressions to give their opinions as they present.

ANSWER KEY

SPEAKING

A–D *(pages 78–79)* Answers will vary.

A *(pages 79–80)*

Read the assignment and the situation aloud as a class. Discuss what kinds of language students will need to use. Some examples include agreeing and disagreeing, asking for and expressing opinions, and talking about priorities. Ask for examples of each type of language from this unit. Have students read about and choose roles as a group.

B **Organizing Ideas** *(page 80)*

Have students time themselves as they practice their talks. Remind them they only have 1 minute to present.

C *(page 80)*

As a class, brainstorm business meeting etiquette before groups present. Examples: Be prepared, sit appropriately, don't look at your phone, and don't interrupt someone while they are speaking or asking a question.

ANSWER KEY

FINAL TASK

A–C *(pages 79–80)* Answers will vary.

REFLECTION

- Have students answer questions 1 and 2 on their own, and then discuss their answers in pairs or small groups.
- Ask students to discuss similarities and differences in their answers for questions 1 and 2.
- For question 3, have students compare answers and then write the words about which they are still unsure on the board. Lead a class review of the challenging words, and reteach terms as necessary.

5   INSIDE THE BRAIN

ACADEMIC TRACK
Psychology

ACADEMIC SKILLS

LISTENING	Listening for Reasons and Explanations
	Recording the Steps in a Process
SPEAKING	Making Suggestions
	Linking
CRITICAL THINKING	Identifying Solutions

UNIT OVERVIEW

This unit presents interesting facts about the human brain. Although science has made many advances in understanding how the brain functions, much about the brain still remains a mystery.

- **LISTENING A** **A Podcast about Exercise and the Brain:** In a podcast, two people discuss the benefits that exercise has on the human brain.

- **VIDEO** ***3-D Brain Scans:*** Dr. Jeff Lichtman and his team at the Lichtman Lab at Harvard University are trying to discover more about the nerve cells in the human brain. Ultrathin slices of mouse brains offer a mesmerizing look at how brain cells communicate on the tiniest scale. This research may offer clues about the inner workings of our own synapses.

- **LISTENING B** **A Discussion about Memory, Learning, and Emotions:** Three classmates in a study group have a discussion about learning, emotions, and the memory process.

For the final task, students draw upon what they have learned in the unit to work in groups and plan a presentation about an aspect of the human brain.

For additional information about the topics in this unit, here are some suggestions for online search terms: *ways to improve memory, structure of the brain, neurons, amygdala, effects of exercise on the brain, BDNF, good study habits, nerve cells, brain scans, Harvard University, dopamine, Obsessive-Compulsive Disorder, short-term memory, long-term memory*

 **UNIT OPENER**

THINK AND DISCUSS *(page 81)*

Direct students' attention to the photo, title, and caption. Ask leading questions, such as:
- Who is the man in this photo? *(Dru-gu Choegyal Rinpoche)*
- What does he do for work? *(a Buddhist teacher and an artist)*

ANSWER KEY

THINK AND DISCUSS *(page 81)*

1. Possible answer: Scientists are studying his brain activity. They might want to study his brain because he's a Buddhist teacher and artist.
2. Answers will vary.

EXPLORE THE THEME *(pages 82–83)*

Have students describe the photos, read the captions, and discuss the questions in small groups. Ask students to describe or demonstrate their answers to question 4 for the class.

ANSWER KEY

EXPLORE THE THEME *(pages 82–83)*

1. Possible answer: The people in these photos are playing chess, running/jogging, juggling, and making pottery. They are doing these activities because they enjoy them, they want to relax, get in shape, and exercise their brains.
2. Possible answers: Chess can improve your memory. Running/jogging can make you feel happier. Pottery can reduce stress.
3. Answers will vary.
4. Possible answer: Doing word and number puzzles, doing yoga, swimming.

Lesson A

VOCABULARY
30 MINS

A 🎧 **2.2** **Meaning from Context** *(page 84)*

Before listening, activate students' prior knowledge by discussing some general questions such as whether everyone's brain is the same and what things affect the development of the brain. After they have listened to the information, ask students which fact they found most interesting or surprising.

Ideas for… CHECKING COMPREHENSION

Check students' understanding with follow-up questions, such as:

- Why is it important to keep learning? (*Learning changes the structure of the brain.*)
- What does the *hypothalamus* do? (*It controls your body temperature.*)
- What do *neurons* do? (*They send messages to your body.*)
- What does the *amygdala* do? (*It lets you read other people's faces and understand their moods.*)

Ideas for… MULTI-LEVEL CLASSES

To make listening exercises more challenging for higher-level students, have them close their books rather than follow along with the text as they listen.

B *(pages 84–85)*

Have students underline the vocabulary word in each question. (**1.** controls; **2.** generate; **3.** signals; **4.** complex; **5.** speeds; **6.** tiny; **7.** connection; **8.** structure; **9.** mood; **10.** functions) Remind them to use the context to work out the meanings of these words.

C **Critical Thinking: Analyzing** *(page 85)*

Draw the chart on the board as students work. Invite volunteers to write their ideas in the chart. Review answers as a class.

Ideas for… EXPANSION

Have students write five new sentences that are true for them using the words in blue from exercise A. Ask them to complete the activity individually then share their sentences in pairs for peer feedback. Students should check their partner's sentences to see if the part of speech is used correctly.

D **Critical Thinking: Analyzing** *(page 85)*

Have volunteers share any culturally specific gestures to express feelings of happiness, to show understanding, and to agree with someone.

Ideas for… EXPANSION

Ask students to look at the photos in this unit and "read" the people's faces. Have them discuss with a partner how those people are feeling and why.

ANSWER KEY

VOCABULARY

B *(pages 84–85)* **1.** need; **2.** can; **3.** will; **4.** many; **5.** quickly; **6.** smallest; **7.** feel; **8.** couldn't; **9.** good; **10.** are

C *(page 85)*

Nouns: signals; speeds; connections; structure; mood; function

Verbs: controls; generates

Adjectives: tiny; complex

D *(page 85)*

1. Answers will vary.
2. Possible answer: It can help you understand how to react to what people say and do.
3. Answers will vary.
4. Possible answers: You can control your diet, your attitude, and how much you exercise. You cannot control where you were born or the features you inherited.

LISTENING: A PODCAST ABOUT EXERCISE AND THE BRAIN

BEFORE LISTENING

A **Predicting** *(page 86)*

Remind students to give reasons for their choices.

Ideas for… EXPANSION

Direct students' attention to the photo on page 87. Ask them to reflect on their own experiences with exercise and the topics in the box. Ask guiding questions, such as: What kind of exercise are they doing in the photo? What kind of exercise do you like to do? How does this affect your mood? How do you think exercise is related to learning or your memory? Give students time to discuss in pairs.

WHILE LISTENING

B [2.3] [1.8] **Listening for Main Ideas** *(page 86)*

Give students time to read the sentences. Play the audio again while students choose their answers.

Ideas for… PRESENTING THE LISTENING SKILL: Listening for Reasons and Explanations

Review the information in the box. Read the common signal phrases aloud so students know what to listen for.

C [2.3] **Listening for Details** *(page 87)*

Have students read through the ideas and reasons or explanations before listening to the podcast and guess the answers. Reviews answers as a class.

Ideas for… CHECKING COMPREHENSION

In pairs, ask students to rewrite the four sentences from exercise C using other signal phrases before giving the reasons and explanations. Encourage them to be creative and add additional information they remember from the podcast or their own experience. For example, *1. Exercise makes it easier to learn. To explain, after doing exercise, such as running or swimming, your body produces a certain chemical that helps your brain stay healthy.*

AFTER LISTENING

D **Critical Thinking: Reflecting** *(page 87)*

List questions students have about the podcast on the board. Ask volunteers to provide answers or ideas.

ANSWER KEY

LISTENING

A *(page 86)* Possible answers:
  Discussed: learning; neurons; mood; memory
  Not discussed: food/taste; brain surgery; intelligence

B *(page 86)* **1.** c; d; **2.** c; **3.** a

C *(page 87)* **1.** d; **2.** b; **3.** a; **4.** c

D *(page 87)* Answers will vary.

 SPEAKING

Ideas for… PRESENTING GRAMMAR FOR SPEAKING: Infinitives after Verbs

Use the following activity to help students practice and remember verbs followed by infinitives. First, dictate the following sentences to students as they write them in their notebooks. Then have students walk around the classroom, asking questions to find the answers. Share answers as a class.

Find someone who…
- wants to learn something new.
- plans to take a vacation.
- hopes to go to college.
- has decided to get married.
- needs to save money.
- wants to learn to play a musical instrument.
- plans to go to a foreign country.
- needs to find a new job.
- hopes to meet someone new.

A *(page 88)*

Allow time for students to complete the sentences individually. Ask volunteers to read their sentences aloud. Accept alternative answers.

B **Personalizing** *(page 88)*

Have students tell the class about their partners, based on each partner's answers. For example, "When Rafael was a child, he wanted …"

C *(pages 88–89)*

Put students in groups of four or five. Review the instructions as a class. Be sure all students understand before playing.

Ideas for… PRESENTING PRONUNCIATION:
Linking

🎧 2.4   Read the information in the box. Explain that linking words in this way will make them sound more fluent and natural. Play the audio. Say the sentences, emphasizing the linked words, and ask students to repeat. Note: The link between *be* and *interesting* in the third example can be described as a /y/ sound.

D 🎧 2.5   *(page 89)*

Play the audio again, and pause so that students can repeat. Go over the answers as a class.

E *(page 89)*

Have volunteers say the sentences aloud for the class.

Ideas for… PRESENTING THE SPEAKING SKILL:
Making Suggestions

Have volunteers read the examples in the box. Ask students for suggestions about who might say these sentences and in what situations.

Ideas for… EXPANSION

Have students do a role-play in pairs. Partner A is a doctor, and Partner B is a patient having trouble remembering things. Ask Partner A, the doctor, to give three different suggestions to help Partner B, the patient, remember things. Remind students to use words and phrases from the *Speaking Skill* box.

F Making Suggestions *(page 90)*

Have students write a dialogue based on another common conversation between two college students.

G Personalizing *(page 90)*

Have volunteers share their problems with the class to get additional suggestions and feedback.

TIP It may be uncomfortable for students to talk about personal problems or difficult situations. In this case, they can make up problems or talk about a friend or a relative.

LESSON TASK: DISCUSSING PROBLEMS AND SOLUTIONS

(35 MINS)

A Critical Thinking: Analyzing *(pages 90–91)*

Call on volunteers to read each of the problems aloud to the class. As a class, brainstorm a few possible solutions for the first problem.

Ideas for... EXPANSION

Have students add one more box to exercise A, giving a short explanation of a problem they have in their personal, academic, or professional life. Remind them to use the current problems as examples of everyday problems. Encourage them to present this problem to their partner in exercise B to brainstorm helpful suggestions for how to solve it.

B Critical Thinking: Applying *(page 91)*

Walk around while students are practicing. Make sure conversations are culturally sensitive and appropriate.

C *(page 91)*

Allow time for students to ask any follow-up or clarification questions after each role-play. Lead a class discussion to evaluate the benefits and challenges of the each solution presented.

ANSWER KEY

LESSON TASK

A–C *(pages 90–91)* Answers will vary.

Video

(45 MINS)

VIEWING: *3-D BRAIN SCANS* *(page 92)*

Overview of the Video

Dr. Jeff Lichtman and his team at the Lichtman Lab at Harvard University are trying to discover more about the nerve cells in the human brain. Ultrathin slices of mouse brains offer a mesmerizing look at how brain cells communicate on the tiniest scale. This research may offer clues about the inner workings of our own synapses.

BEFORE VIEWING

A *(page 92)*

Ask students to record these words in their vocabulary journals using new example sentences.

Ideas for... CHECKING COMPREHENSION

Check students' understanding with follow-up questions, such as:

- What is a way of greeting people that is unconventional for you?
- What is the age gap between your parents? Between your brothers or sisters?
- If you had to map out the next three to five years of your life, what events would be detailed?
- What is something you have a difficult time keeping track of?

B Critical Thinking: Analyzing *(page 92)*

Read the information aloud as a class. Give students 5 minutes to discuss it.

WHILE VIEWING

C ▶ 1.9 Understanding Main Ideas *(page 93)*

Give students time to read the summary and guess the answers before watching the video.

D ▶ 1.9 Understanding Details *(page 93)*

Have students compare answers. Play the video (or parts of the video) again, if necessary.

E **Critical Thinking: Analyzing** *(page 93)*

Remind students to support their opinions with reasons or examples.

ANSWER KEY

VIDEO

A *(page 92)* **1.** b; **2.** d; **3.** a; **4.** c

B *(page 92)* Possible answer:

The nerve cells are long and thin like wires, and they carry electrical signals like wires do.

C *(page 93)* **1.** the person is acting; **2.** nothing to see; **3.** see the wires; **4.** communicate with each other; **5.** slices; **6.** millimeter; **7.** in sequence; **8.** cell

D *(page 93)*

1. don't know/have no idea

2. space

3. no meaning

E *(page 93)*

1. Possible answer: It is difficult because scientists cannot easily examine human brains or do experiments on them.

2. Answers will vary.

3. Possible answers: Is it possible to make conclusions about the human brain from studies on mice brains? Do all human brains have the same number of "wires"?

Lesson B

30 MINS

VOCABULARY

A 🎧 2.6 **Meaning from Context** *(page 94)*

To activate prior knowledge, ask students to think of some people they love. Ask "Why do you love them?"

> **Ideas for… PRESENTING THE VOCABULARY SKILL: Using Context Clues**
>
> Ask students to work in pairs, look back at the article, and find one additional example of each type of clue.

B *(page 95)*

Have pairs form groups of four and compare the context clues they found.

C *(page 95)*

Have students complete the exercise individually. Review answers as a class.

> **Ideas for… EXPANSION**
>
> Have students reflect on of the different kinds of love in their life. Ask them to find and show photos of their loved ones to a partner and describe their relationships using the target vocabulary and other ideas from the article in exercise A on page 94. Give an example from your own life. For example: This is my mother. When I am with my mother, I have feelings of security and trust.

LESSON B: VOCABULARY

B *(page 95)* Possible answers:

There are many different kinds of love. There is the strong **emotion** <u>we feel</u> when we fall in love. There is the **attachment** <u>between parents and children</u>, and the quiet feeling of **security** that develops slowly in **long-term** relationships, when couples are <u>together for many years</u>.

Your brain knows the difference between **romantic** <u>love and other attachments</u>. When <u>we're in love</u>, the amount of a brain chemical called *dopamine* increases. This increase gives us the extra energy we feel when we're in love.

On the other hand, an increase in dopamine can make the brains of people in love **similar** to the brains of people with OCD—Obsessive Compulsive Disorder. People with OCD cannot stop thinking about something, and these thoughts can cause compulsive behaviors—<u>actions the person cannot control</u>, such as washing the hands again and again. Similarly, people who are in love often cannot stop thinking about the person they are in love with. Both kinds of people may find it difficult to **function** normally because of their thoughts.

Fortunately, this "lovesickness" is a **short-term** condition. With time, strong romantic feelings decrease, and we can **concentrate** on "real life" again. As time passes, couples have higher levels of *oxytocin*—<u>a brain chemical connected with calm feelings</u> of happiness and trust.

So is love only a matter of brain chemistry? In fact, while chemicals do affect the way we feel, **psychological** factors are also important. We might be attracted to someone who <u>likes the same things we like</u>, for example, or someone who <u>makes us feel safe and secure</u>.

C *(page 95)* **1.** long-term; **2.** similar; **3.** attachment; **4.** concentrate; **5.** emotion; **6.** function; **7.** psychological; **8.** romantic; **9.** short-term; **10.** security

LISTENING: A DISCUSSION ABOUT MEMORY, LEARNING, AND EMOTIONS

BEFORE LISTENING

A *(page 96)*

Have volunteers share things they remember with short-term versus long-term memory. Write ideas on the board, and come up with a class definition for each term.

WHILE LISTENING

B 🎧 2.7 **Listening for Main Ideas** *(page 96)*

Give students time to read the sentences before listening to the discussion so they know what main ideas to listen for.

C 🎧 2.7 **Listening for Details** *(page 96)*

Have volunteers share ideas to correct the false statements.

> Ideas for… **PRESENTING THE NOTE-TAKING SKILL:** Recording the Steps in a Process
>
> Elicit examples from students of different personal, professional, or academic situations in which this type of note taking would be useful.

> Ideas for… **EXPANSION**
>
> Think of something you do well. Explain to a partner how to complete this activity, step by step. Then switch roles and take notes as you listen to your partner's explanation.

D 🎧 2.8 **Note Taking** *(page 97)*

Review answers as a class. Have each student retell the steps in the process to a partner without looking at his or her notes.

AFTER LISTENING

E Personalizing *(page 97)*

Before students discuss, brainstorm vocabulary related to emotions with the class. Elicit examples from students and write their ideas on the board (*stressed, relaxed, anxious, afraid, joyful, angry, excited,* etc.) Encourage them to use the words as a reference for question 3. Have students demonstrate different strategies or recommend resources to remember new vocabulary.

TIP Mnemonic devices are strategies that help students improve their memory of words and phrases by connecting new information to prior knowledge through the use of visual and/or acoustic cues. Whenever possible, encourage students use mnemonic devices to associate new words with images, rhymes or songs, or any information based on their own life experience.

F Critical Thinking: Reflecting *(page 97)*

Ask students to reflect on what is true for them and answer the questions individually before sharing in pairs. Remind them to give real-life examples to explain their opinions. Model question 1 for the class. Say: For question 1, I circled the number 1 because I strongly disagree! When I was younger, I had a lot of difficulty learning new skills like playing the piano. Now that I'm older, I have more confidence, and this helps me learn more easily.

ANSWER KEY

LISTENING

A *(page 96)* Answers will vary.

B *(page 96)* **1.** function normally; **2.** can last; **3.** think about; **4.** chemical

C *(page 96)* **1.** F (The memory process has <u>three</u> steps.); **2.** F (Memories become <u>stronger</u> when they travel down the same pathway many times.); **3.** T; **4.** T; **5.** F (The level of dopamine in our brains <u>increases</u> when we fall in love.)

D *(page 97)*

Step 1: information, senses

Step 2: to use, short-term, to answer

Step 3: to remember, brain, important, long-term

E–F *(page 97)* Answers will vary.

 **SPEAKING**

A Critical Thinking: Analyzing *(page 98)*

Invite students to share their feelings about and personal experiences with group work. Ask "Why do you think so many teachers assign group work? Why is it important? What does it help students learn?"

Ideas for… MULTI-LEVEL CLASSES

Arrange students in same-level partners for the exercises in the Speaking section. Students may feel more comfortable sharing their ideas about group work with a student who is at a similar level.

B *(page 98)*

Ask volunteers to write ideas of other tasks on the board and provide examples of fair ways to divide the research work.

C *(page 98)*

Discuss one or two benefits or possible problems as a class. Allow time for students to work in pairs to complete the chart.

D Critical Thinking: Identifying Solutions *(page 99)*

Choose one of the potential problems and complete steps 1 and 2 as a class. Arrange the pairs in mixed-level groups of four to complete the exercise.

ANSWER KEY

LESSON B: SPEAKING

A–D *(pages 98–99)* Answers will vary.

FINAL TASK: PLANNING A PRESENTATION ABOUT THE HUMAN BRAIN

A *(page 99)*

Read through the questions as a class. Clarify any confusing language or ideas. Tell students to share with their group what role they prefer to take in group work and what they feel they do best.

TIP Give students time to try to answer all the questions in exercise A before choosing just one to focus on for their presentation. The group's initial assumption about which question they can best answer may be challenged after exploring all the topics.

B Critical Thinking: Evaluating *(page 100)*

Make sure all students are carrying out their roles as they participate in the discussion.

C Organizing Ideas *(page 100)*

Suggest that students practice several times. They can record their presentations on a phone or online and give each other feedback as they watch them with their group members.

D Presenting *(page 100)*

Encourage students to share tips on different ways to conduct research and how and where to find interesting visuals. Create a class resource list that students can access online.

> **Ideas for... PRESENTING THE PRESENTATION SKILL: Pausing to Check Understanding**
>
> Explain to students that pauses are a powerful presentation skill that help listeners process ideas and give speakers the chance to gauge the audience's response and interest. Teach students to pause before beginning a presentation, after a question, when transitioning between ideas, and when needed for emphasis. Suggest that they pause and then count to three in their head before moving on. Model speaking with and without pauses to demonstrate the difference.

E *(page 100)*

Give students a date by which their presentations should be ready. You may want to spread the presentations over two or three classes.

ANSWER KEY

FINAL TASK

A–E *(pages 99–100)* Answers will vary.

REFLECTION

- Have students answer questions 1 and 2 on their own, and then discuss answers in pairs or small groups.
- Ask students to discuss similarities and differences in their answers for questions 1 and 2.
- For question 3, have students compare answers and then write the words about which they are still unsure on the board. Lead a class review of the challenging words, and reteach terms as necessary.

LET'S EAT!

6

<table>
<tr><td>

ACADEMIC TRACK
Health & Nutrition

ACADEMIC SKILLS
LISTENING	Listening for Numerical Data
	Using a Split Page to Take Notes
SPEAKING	Interrupting and Returning to a Topic
	Intonation: Finished and Unfinished Sentences
CRITICAL THINKING	Evaluating

UNIT OVERVIEW

This unit explores some interesting facts about food and diet. Eating habits are changing in many countries, and it is important to be aware of the effects of these changes on health.

- **LISTENING A A Presentation about the Korean Diet:** A student gives a seminar presentation about changes to the South Korean diet between 1969 and 1995.

- **VIDEO *The Food and Culture of Oaxaca:*** Learn about the rich traditional culture of the city and state of Oaxaca in Mexico, with a particular focus on its world-famous food.

- **LISTENING B A Discussion about Food Psychology:** Friends engage in a discussion about the ways that food psychology is used to appeal to customers.

For the final task, students draw upon what they have learned in the unit to present a marketing plan for a food truck, including ideas for attracting and appealing to customers.

For additional information about the topics in this unit, here are some suggestions for online search terms: *Bailongtan Temple Fair, worldwide diet, nutritional guidelines, typical Korean diet, vegetarian versus omnivorous diet, Oaxaca Mexico, mole, Guelagetza, Dr. Alia Crum milkshake experiment, ghrelin, food psychology*

</td><td>

 **UNIT OPENER**

THINK AND DISCUSS *(page 101)*

Direct students' attention to the photo, title, and caption. Ask leading questions, such as:
- Who are the people in the photo? Where are they from? *(maybe family and friends; from China)*
- Where are they? *(Bailongtan Temple Fair in Anyang, Henan Province, China)*
- What are they eating? *(noodles)*

ANSWER KEY

THINK AND DISCUSS *(page 101)*

1. Possible answer: The people in the photo are eating noodles from a huge pot.
2.–3. Answers will vary.

EXPLORE THE THEME *(pages 102–103)*

Ask students questions to check their understanding of what the pie chart is about, such as:
- What is it comparing? *(the world's daily diet in calories)*
- How does it compare them? *(It shows the total daily calories of an average diet around the world and how many calories are obtained from each food group.)*

Review the questions. Ask students to create a food chart similar to the one on page 103 for their own typical daily diet and compare it with their classmates' food charts.

Ideas for... EXPANSION

In pairs, have students brainstorm examples of food for each category represented in the pie chart.

ANSWER KEY

EXPLORE THE THEME *(pages 102–103)*

1. The foods shown in the photos are fish and bread. Answers to second question will vary.
2. People get more of their calories from fruits and vegetables than from meat.
3.–4. Answers will vary.

</td></tr>
</table>

45

Lesson A

 VOCABULARY

A 🎧 **2.9** *(page 104)*

Ask students to look at the photo and name the vegetables and fruits they recognize. Review definitions of any new vocabulary words as a class.

B 🎧 **2.10** **Meaning from Context** *(page 104)*

Do the first sentence with the class as an example. Set a time limit for students to complete the exercise.

C **Personalizing** *(page 105)*

Review the questions and adverbs in the quiz. Explain how to come up with an explanation or example (e.g., add details, list specific foods, give reasons). Call on volunteers to read one or two of their answers aloud.

D **Critical Thinking: Analyzing** *(page 105)*

Ask students to discuss the questions in pairs and summarize the main points of their discussion for the class.

ANSWER KEY

VOCABULARY

B *(page 104)* **1.** guidelines; **2.** recommend; **3.** Grains; **4.** servings; **5.** source; **6.** regional; **7.** varied; **8.** protein; **9.** specific; **10.** modernize

C *(page 105)* Possible answers:
1. Usually: I eat several kinds of foods every week.
2. Usually: I eat bread with every meal.
3. Sometimes: I try to eat a vegetable at dinner and a piece of fruit for a snack every day.
4. Sometimes: I try to eat in a healthy way, but sometimes I eat too many sweets.
5. Sometimes: I don't like to eat a lot of meat, but I eat dairy products and nuts.
6. Usually: I carry a water bottle with me everywhere I go.
7. Sometimes: I love cheese, but I don't like yogurt.
8. Never: I never check food labels before I buy things at the store.

D *(page 105)*
1.–2. Answers will vary.

---

3. Possible answer: The food is less fresh and local, and people eat faster because they are busier.
4. Possible answers: A varied diet is healthier. If you eat just a few kinds of food, you will not get enough nutrients.
5. Possible answers: Because they may not have a lot of choices and because they may not have enough money.

⏱ **LISTENING: A PRESENTATION ABOUT THE KOREAN DIET**

BEFORE LISTENING

A **Prior Knowledge** *(page 106)*

Encourage students to make a timeline to help them explain how the diet has changed. Remind students to refer to the photo on page 106 as they discuss the foods eaten in South Korea.

Ideas for… MULTI-LEVEL CLASSES

Higher-level students can conduct further research on how their country's diet has changed and write a short paragraph based on their findings. Remind them to use the appropriate verb tenses.

WHILE LISTENING

B 🎧 **2.11** ▶ **1.10** **Listening for Main Ideas** *(page 106)*

Review the information in the box as a class. Ask about students' experiences attending seminars. Give them time to read the questions and make predictions about changes in the Korean diet before listening.

C *(page 106)*

Review answers as a class. If possible, show before and after photos of Korea and Koreans in 1969 and 1995.

Ideas for… PRESENTING THE LISTENING SKILL: Listening for Numerical Data

Discuss different ways to take notes on numerical data. Review the examples in the skill box. Say a variety of sentences that include numerical data. You can talk about important historical events, birthdays, recipes, measurements, mathematics, phone numbers, etc. Ask students to take notes as you speak.

SPEAKING

Sell your books at
sellbackyourBook.com!
Go to sellbackyourBook.com
and get an instant price
quote. We even pay the
shipping - see what your old
books are worth today!

Inspected By: esther_delacruz

00069758707

8707

000697⁵⁷⁵

C-2
S-5

Change in Korean Eating Habits

Kind of Food	Ounces per Day in 1969	Ounces per Day in 1995
Total Food	37	39
Rice and Other Grains	20	11
Vegetables	9.5 (or 9 ½)	10
Fruits	2	5
Meat	.25 (or 1/4)	2.5 (or 2 ½)
Milk and Other Dairy Products	.1 (or 1/10)	2.3

E *(page 107)*

1. Answers will vary.

2. The greatest decrease was in rice and other grains. The greatest increase was in meat.

3.–5. Answers will vary.

Ideas for… PRESENTING GRAMMAR FOR SPEAKING: The Real Conditional: Present and Future

Review the information in the box. Remind students that the meaning remains the same if the clauses are reversed. Point out that we don't use a comma if the main clause comes first. Have students practice reversing the clauses in each example. For example: *I eat chocolate if I have it in the house.*

A *(page 108)*

Encourage students to vary the order of the clauses. Have volunteers write their answers on the board.

B *(page 108)*

Have students ask their partners questions using the prompts. For example, *"What happens if you eat a lot of sugar?"*

C Personalizing *(page 109)*

Have students change partners. After the exercise, have them stand up and ask different classmates questions using the prompts. For example, *"What do you do when you have an important exam?"*

Ideas for… PRESENTING THE SPEAKING SKILL: Interrupting and Returning to a Topic

Ask students for examples of situations in which they might need to interrupt a speaker; for example, when they don't understand something or if they have an important point to add. Read the expressions in the box aloud, exaggerating the rising intonation in the questions. Ask students to repeat.

Ideas for… EXPANSION

In a small group, have students share any gestures, facial expressions, or other body language that people use to interrupt a speaker. Have volunteers demonstrate for the class.

D 🎧 2.12 *(page 109)*

Have volunteers read the excerpts from the presentation aloud as you review the answers.

> Ideas for…**PRESENTING PRONUNCIATION:**
> Intonation: Finished and Unfinished Sentences
>
> 🎧 2.13 Play the audio, and ask students to repeat the examples. Mention that it is often considered impolite to interrupt before a speaker has finished, even when we have a question or an important point to make.

E 🎧 2.14 *(page 110)*

Ask students to mark the rising or falling intonation of each sentence as they listen. Review answers as a class. Have volunteers read sentences aloud with correct intonation.

F *(page 110)*

Point out that sentence *a* has rising intonation and sentence *b* has falling intonation. Encourage students to practice both as they work in pairs. Give them time to make up their own examples.

G **Critical Thinking: Analyzing** *(page 110)*

If possible, have each student work with a partner from the same cultural background. Have each pair share their answers with the class, teaching when it is and isn't appropriate to interrupt in their culture.

TIP If students do not have direct experience with American culture, they should compare their culture with another culture they know well.

ANSWER KEY

SPEAKING

A *(page 108)*

1. If I don't eat breakfast, I feel very hungry by late morning.
2. If I arrive late to class, I enter the room quietly.
3. If my sister sees fresh oranges, she always wants to buy some.
4. If you don't like fish, you shouldn't order that dish.
5. If I feel hungry at night, I sometimes order a pizza.
6. If people don't like to eat meat, they can become vegetarians.

B *(page 108)* Possible answers:

1. You won't have healthy teeth if you eat a lot of sugar.
2. If you drink coffee late at night, you won't be able to fall asleep.
3. If children eat a lot of fast food, they are going to have too much salt in their diet.
4. If you don't eat enough fruits and vegetables, you won't get enough vitamins in your diet.
5. If people learn how to cook, they'll eat better meals for the rest of their lives.
6. If I eat a very big lunch, I'll feel sleepy all afternoon.

C *(page 109)* Answers will vary.

D *(page 109)*

1. Mi-Ran, <u>may I say something here</u>?
2. <u>Moving on</u> . . . when we compare the kinds of food people ate, we see a significant difference.
3. <u>Could I ask a question</u>, Mi-Ran?
4. <u>To continue</u>—as the country developed, instead of just eating a lot of rice and vegetables, Koreans started including many other kinds of foods in their diets,. . .

E *(page 110)* **1.** F; **2.** U; **3.** U; **4.** F; **5.** U; **6.** F

G *(page 110)* Answers will vary.

LESSON TASK: PARTICIPATING IN A GROUP DISCUSSION
35 MINS

A Brainstorming *(page 111)*

While students are brainstorming, walk around the classroom, and check their work to make sure they understand how a reason (cause), an explanation (clarification), and an example (specific case or situation) differ. Encourage students to use both facts and personal experience to support their opinion.

B Critical Thinking: Evaluating *(page 111)*

Ask students to write their ideas in a list. Have them cross off the ones they aren't going to use and circle the ones they are going to use. Put an example on the board.

C *(page 111)*

Emphasize that this activity is like a competitive debate between teams: they don't necessarily give their real opinions.

D *(page 111)*

Ask students what it was like to debate an opinion that wasn't theirs. Draw a T-chart on the board, and have volunteers list reasons why they believe one diet is better than the other. Have a class debate.

> **ANSWER KEY**
>
> **LESSON TASK** *(page 111)*
> **A–D** Answers will vary.

Video

VIEWING: *THE FOOD AND CULTURE OF OAXACA* *(page 112)*
45 MINS

Overview of the Video

Learn about the rich traditional culture of the city and state of Oaxaca in Mexico, with a particular focus on its world-famous food.

BEFORE VIEWING

A Prior Knowledge *(page 112)*

Have students share which Mexican foods they have tried and whether they liked them.

B Predicting *(page 112)*

Write all the words students come up with on the board.

WHILE VIEWING

C ▶ 1.11 Checking Predictions *(page 112)*

Play the video, and circle any words on the board from the previous exercise that are mentioned.

D ▶ 1.11 Understanding Details *(page 112)*

Have students discuss their answers in pairs before going over the exercise as a class.

E ▶ 1.11 Understanding Details *(page 113)*

Have students guess which words complete the sentences before listening. Have volunteers read the sentences aloud to review answers as a class.

AFTER VIEWING

F Personalizing *(page 113)*

Encourage students to think about the information in the video and relate it to their own experience.

G *(page 113)*

Set a time limit for this exercise, and go over the answers as a class.

Lesson B

VOCABULARY
30 MINS

A 🎧 2.15 **Meaning from Context** *(page 114)*

Have students form groups of three and complete a jigsaw pre-reading activity before listening. Each group member is assigned the introduction, the results, or the discussion. Give students 5 minutes to read and take notes on the main points in their sections. Then have each student present his or her section to the group.

> **Ideas for… CHECKING FOR COMPREHENSION**
>
> Check for students' understanding of Dr. Alia Crum's milkshake experiment by asking questions, such as:
> - Who is Dr. Crum? *(a psychologist and researcher)*
> - What was the objective of the experiment? *(to find out whether reading food labels affects the body)*
> - What does the hormone *ghrelin* do? *(stimulates feelings of hunger when we need to eat)*
> - How did the experiment work? *(Two groups drank the same milkshake with different food labels, rated the taste, and took a blood test to measure ghrelin levels.)*
> - What were the results? *(Attitude is relevant to the way our bodies respond to food.)*

B *(page 115)*

Challenge students to try to complete the exercise without looking at the article in exercise A.

C Personalizing *(page 115)*

Remind students that effective follow-up questions are open-ended *wh-* questions.

> **Ideas for… PRESENTING THE VOCABULARY SKILL:**
> Recognizing Parts of Speech
>
> Review the functions of a noun and verb. Have students find examples of other nouns and verbs in the article in exercise A, and point out the context clues that helped them identify the part of speech.

D Critical Thinking: Analyzing *(page 115)*

Have volunteers read the sentences aloud to review the answers. Remind them to give reasons for their choices.

LISTENING: A DISCUSSION ABOUT FOOD PSYCHOLOGY

BEFORE LISTENING

A *(page 116)*

Ask a volunteer to read the information in the box aloud. Lead a class discussion to review answers.

WHILE LISTENING

> **Ideas for… PRESENTING THE NOTE-TAKING SKILL:**
> Using a Split Page to Take Notes
>
> Ask students whether they think this note-taking skill will be helpful for them and why.

B 🎧 **2.16** **Note Taking** *(page 117)*

Give students time to read the partial notes before listening so they know what to listen for. Remind them to focus only on the right-hand side of the split page.

C 🎧 **2.16** **Note Taking** *(page 117)*

Have students listen again, and remind them to focus only on the right-hand side of the split page.

AFTER LISTENING

D *(page 117)*

Walk around as students work, and provide help with question formation and vocabulary as needed.

E *(page 117)*

Review students' questions and main notes as a class. Ask volunteers to write their questions on the board.

F Critical Thinking: Analyzing *(page 117)*

Have three different volunteers take turns reading the information in the box aloud. Help with pronunciation issues as they come up. If possible, show photos of the food and flavor trends as students read and discuss.

> **Ideas for… EXPANSION**
>
> Have students work in pairs to find and analyze an advertisement online or in a magazine for a food or drink product. Have pairs form a group of four. Ask each pair to show the advertisement to their group and explain how the company uses food psychology to convince people to buy its product.

LISTENING

A *(page 116)* Answers will vary.

B *(page 117)* Possible answers:

> **Main Notes**
>
> *Food psychology:*
> - *descriptions and photos of food on menus* appeal to hungry people OR stimulate your appetite
> - *survey cards give customers a chance* to give feedback and rate the food and service
> - *social connections (i.e., getting together for a meal with* friends, family, neighbors *)*
> - *a variety of foods/having many options (e.g., at grocery store) makes us* want to buy one of everything

C *(page 117)* Answers will vary.

D *(page 117)* Possible answers:

> *Questions*
>
> *How do restaurants appeal to hungry people?*
>
> *Possible question:*
>
> *Why do restaurants use survey cards?*
> *What other kinds of communication are important?*
> *Possible question:*
> *Why do grocery stores display a huge variety of foods?*

F *(page 117)*

1. Answers will vary.
2. Possible answer: Food psychology is used to make certain foods appeal to us. Tropical fruits are colorful and fun. This might appeal to people in North America because they don't see them regularly, so they are new and interesting.
3. Answers will vary.

 **SPEAKING**

A **Critical Thinking: Analyzing** *(page 118)*

Lead a class discussion. Write students' ideas for question 2 on the board for future reference.

B 🎧 **2.17** *(page 118)*

Give students time to read the information. Ask them to underline any unfamiliar words. Review the new vocabulary as a class before listening.

C **Critical Thinking: Evaluating** *(page 119)*

Remind students to use everyday language for managing a group discussion as they work.

D *(page 119)*

Have volunteers report their group's conclusions. Rank the tips on the board as a class.

SPEAKING

A *(page 118)*

1. Answers will vary.
2. Possible answer: One advantage of owning a food truck is that you can move it around to where there are the most people at any time. One disadvantage is it isn't as large as a traditional restaurant. Also, it doesn't offer seating.

B–D *(pages 118–119)* Answers will vary.

FINAL TASK: PRESENTING A MARKETING PLAN

35 MINS

A *(page 119)*

Read the assignment aloud. Ask students to describe what a marketing plan is and why it's important for businesses to have one. Have volunteers write their ideas for different kinds of food trucks on the board.

B Critical Thinking: Evaluating *(page 119)*

Allow students to take their time. Remind them to think about the advantages and disadvantages of each kind of food truck and whether it is better or worse than other options listed in the box in exercise A.

C *(page 119)*

Encourage students to look at examples of menus and food descriptions from other restaurants and food trucks for ideas.

> **Ideas for... PRESENTING THE PRESENTATION**
> **SKILL:** Starting Strong
>
> Have a volunteer read the introduction from the presentation in Lesson A aloud. Ask students whether they thought this presentation started strong. Have them brainstorm other possible techniques the presenter could have used to get the attention of the audience at the start of her presentation.

D Organizing Ideas *(page 120)*

Walk around as students work, and check for strong introductions and complete outlines.

E Presenting *(page 120)*

Provide students with a time limit and criteria for assessing each presentation. Remember to allow time for interruptions and follow-up questions and answers.

REFLECTION

- Have students answer questions 1 and 2 on their own, and then discuss their answers in pairs or small groups.
- Ask students to discuss similarities and differences in their answers for questions 1 and 2.
- For question 3, have students compare answers and then write the words about which they are still unsure on the board. Lead a class review of the challenging words, and re-teach terms as necessary.

OUR ACTIVE EARTH

ACADEMIC TRACK

Earth Science

ACADEMIC SKILLS

LISTENING	Listening for Transitions
	Using a Chart to Take Notes
SPEAKING	Using Transitions
	Syllable Number and Syllable Stress Review
CRITICAL THINKING	Predicting Exam Questions

UNIT OVERVIEW

This unit explores some interesting facts about earthquakes and volcanoes. Natural disasters are a fascinating topic of scientific interest, but they are also very dangerous and cause a great deal of damage.

- **LISTENING A An Earth Science Lecture:** A professor gives a lecture about plate tectonics and the different types of tectonic boundaries

- **VIDEO *Volcano Trek*:** A research expedition to the Erta Ale volcano in Ethiopia features National Geographic Explorers Dr. Franck Tessier and Dr. Irene Margaritis. Erta Ale is located at one of the lowest points on Earth and houses the oldest lava lake in the world.

- **LISTENING B A Discussion about Volcanoes:** Students in a study group engage in a discussion about volcanoes and what kinds of questions might be on an upcoming exam.

For the final task, students draw upon what they have learned in the unit to give an individual presentation about a natural disaster.

For additional information about the topics in this unit, here are some suggestions for online search terms: *Mount Pinatubo, San Andreas Fault, tectonic boundaries, Aceh Sumatra Indonesia, Kirikiri Beach, March 2011 tsunami, Erta Ale volcano, Dr. Franck Tessier and Dr. Irene Margaritis, Pacific Ring of Fire, Mount Nyiragongo, Versoix Lake Geneva*

 **UNIT OPENER**

THINK AND DISCUSS *(page 121)*

Direct students' attention to the photo, title, and caption. Ask leading questions, such as:

- Where was this photo taken? *(Mount Pinatubo in the Philippines)*
- Do you think there are people in the car? How are they feeling? *(afraid; helpless)*

ANSWER KEY

THINK AND DISCUSS *(page 121)*

1. Mount Pinatubo is erupting.
2. Possible answers: Mount St. Helens, Washington, USA; Sakurajima, Japan; Mount Vesuvius, Italy
3. Possible answers: volcanoes, hurricanes, floods, and other natural disasters

EXPLORE THE THEME *(pages 122–123)*

Have students look at the map and discuss the questions in small groups. Ask volunteers to share their reactions to the photos and information about volcanoes and earthquakes with the class.

ANSWER KEY

EXPLORE THE THEME *(pages 122–123)*

1. Possible answer: The San Andreas Fault is located in California. It is the boundary line of two tectonic plates. Earthquakes are frequent there as a result.
2. The color red means very high hazard. It shows where earthquakes are most likely to occur.
3. Earthquakes are most likely to occur in Peru, Chile, California, Alaska, Pakistan, Indonesia, Japan, New Zealand, Haiti, and Mexico. Earthquakes are least likely to occur in most of Africa, Brazil, and Canada, as well as in Madagascar, Russia, and the Midwest and East in the United States.
4. Answers will vary.

Lesson A

30 MINS

VOCABULARY

A [2.18] **Meaning from Context** *(page 124)*

Play the audio while students read. Check their understanding by asking follow-up questions, such as:

- How would you describe tectonic plates? *(pieces of Earth's outer layer that are always moving)*
- What are earthquake zones? *(regions where earthquakes are more likely to occur)*
- What's one reason many people die in earthquakes? *(unsafe buildings)*

B *(page 125)*

Have students complete the exercise individually and then form pairs to compare answers.

C *(page 125)*

Ask students to first identify the part of speech for each of the words in blue in exercise A. Remind them to use this information and other context clues to complete exercise C.

D **Critical Thinking: Analyzing** *(page 125)*

Ask students which building they would feel most safe in. Remind them to give reasons for their choice.

TIP Some students may not feel comfortable talking about potentially traumatic events because of past experiences. Be aware of students' reactions, and allow them to listen rather than discuss if they prefer not to share.

ANSWER KEY

VOCABULARY

B *(page 125)* **1.** T; **2.** F (It does move.); **3.** F (It means they are not killed.); **4.** T; **5.** F (When you construct something, you put it up or build it.); **6.** T; **7.** T; **8.** F (We reinforce walls to make them stronger.); **9.** T; **10.** T

C *(page 125)* **1.** collapse; **2.** construct, reinforce; **3.** survive; **4.** shakes; **5.** materials; **6.** zone; **7.** boundaries; **8.** earthquake; **9.** major

D *(page 125)*

1. Possible answer: The first house has light walls which are less likely to fall to the ground. The second house has light roofs which won't collapse and small windows to keep walls stronger. The third house uses plastic to reinforce the walls. The fourth house uses concrete and metal rods to hold together brick walls.

2.–3. Answers will vary.

LISTENING: AN EARTH SCIENCE LECTURE

BEFORE LISTENING

A Critical Thinking: Interpreting A Map
(page 126)

Ask students to look at the map and predict what the listening will be about.

WHILE LISTENING

B 🎧 2.19 ▶ 1.12 Listening for Main Ideas
(page 126)

Tell students they are going to listen to an Earth Science lecture. Write on the board: *Earth Science is the study of …* Ask volunteers to complete the sentence. *(Earth Science is the study of Earth and its atmosphere.)*

Ideas for… PRESENTING THE NOTE-TAKING SKILL: Using a Chart to Take Notes

Ask students to list and compare the different types of note-taking charts they've learned about so far (e.g., T-charts, a split page, a numbered list). Have them discuss the following questions in small groups: How do you decide which type of chart to use in your notes? Which type of chart has been the most useful for you? Why?

C 🎧 2.19 Note Taking (page 127)

Help students to interpret the chart. Ask students to fill in any information they remember before listening to the audio again.

AFTER LISTENING

D Critical Thinking: Predicting Exam Questions (page 127)

Discuss and show examples of different types of exam questions such as short-answer, multiple-choice, matching, and essay. Make sure students' questions can be answered from information presented in the text.

E Critical Thinking: Analyzing (page 127)

Remind students to refer to their notes to answer their classmate's exam questions.

LISTENING

A *(page 126)*

1. The colors represent the probable strength of earthquakes in the area.
2. The green lines on the map represent tectonic plates.
3. Possible answers: Chile, Peru, California, U.S.A., Pakistan, and Indonesia

B *(page 126)*

1. plate tectonics
2. the places where the earth's plates meet
3. three
4. Possible answer: The buildings were constructed in the right way for earthquake zones.

C *(page 127)*

Boundary Type	Convergent	Divergent	Transform
Movement	Plates come together; one plate can move under or over another.	Plates move apart.	Plates move past each other.
Results	Mountains are formed; mountains are pushed higher.	A body of water can form between the two plates.	Earthquakes can occur when plates "jump."

D *(page 127)* Possible answers:

1. Define convergent boundaries and describe what happens at those boundaries.
2. Contrast convergent and divergent boundaries.
3. Along what type of boundaries do earthquakes occur?
4. Which type of boundary can result in the formation of bodies of water?
5. What kinds of buildings improve people's chances of survival during earthquakes?

SPEAKING

**Ideas for… PRESENTING THE SPEAKING SKILL:
Using Transitions**

After students have read the information in the chart, ask the following questions: Which type of transition shows that two pieces of information are different? (*contrast*) Which type shows similarities? (*addition*) Which type introduces specific ideas? (*example*) Which type shows that one event happens because of another? (*result*) Elicit other examples of common transitions for each category, and write them on the board.

A *(page 128)*

Ask volunteers to read their answers aloud. Note that there are two possible answers for each sentence.

B *(page 129)*

Have each student work with a different partner. Ask students what they know about preparation for extreme weather emergencies. Write their ideas on the board.

**Ideas for… PRESENTING GRAMMAR FOR
SPEAKING: Gerunds as Subjects and Objects**

Compare examples of gerunds with examples of present continuous verbs to demonstrate the difference in form between the two. Point out the position of the gerund in the subject and object examples.

Ideas for… EXPANSION

Have students work individually to write five sentences about things they avoid, things they miss, and things they suggest others do. Then have them share their sentences with partners.

C *(page 130)*

For each question, have students write "S" if the gerund is the subject of the sentence or "O" if it is the object of a verb or preposition. (Answers: **1.** S; **2.** O; **3.** O; **4.** S; **5.** O; **6.** O)

D *(page 130)*

Encourage students to continue their conversations by asking follow-up questions.

E Critical Thinking: Applying *(page 130)*

Have volunteers tell the class about their partners. Challenge them to present without their notes.

ANSWER KEY

SPEAKING

A *(page 128)*
1. Therefore/As a result
2. However/On the other hand
3. For instance/For example
4. In addition/Furthermore
5. Therefore/As a result

B *(page 129)* Possible answers:
1. We <u>do</u> live in an earthquake zone. Therefore, <u>we need to be prepared for earthquakes</u>.
2. For instance, <u>we sometimes have typhoons</u>.
3. Furthermore, <u>I always have bottled water in the refrigerator</u>.
4. On the other hand, <u>I know how to stay safe if one occurs</u>.
5. In addition, <u>public transportation might not be available</u>.
6. As a result, <u>many people and animals died</u>.

C *(page 130)* **1.** Predicting; **2.** being; **3.** going; **4.** Having; **5.** repeating; **6.** getting

D *(page 130)* Answers will vary.

LESSON TASK: INTERVIEWING A PARTNER ABOUT AN EXPERIENCE

A [2.20] *(pages 130–131)*

Have a volunteer read the information in the box on page 131 aloud. Ask students whether they remember this earthquake. Have them share their memories in pairs. After the listening, review answers as a class.

B **Critical Thinking: Analyzing** *(page 131)*

Have each pair write down five questions they think Chaskielberg asked the people in the photo.

Ideas for... EXPANSION

Ask students to consider the following questions: When a tragedy occurs, such as a tsunami that destroys people's homes, should photographers take photos? How do you think photos of tragedies affect people? How do you think they affect the photographer? Have students work with the same partners they had for exercise B.

C *(page 131)*

Allow students to share a difficult experience of a friend or family member if they are not comfortable sharing a personal experience. Make sure students know ahead of time that their partners will explain the experience they share to a group.

D **Critical Thinking: Applying** *(page 131)*

Set a time limit for each student to talk about his or her partner's experience.

ANSWER KEY

LESSON TASK

A *(pages 130–131)* **1.** Living, knowing; **2.** thinking; **3.** helping; **4.** Traveling; **5.** returning; **6.** taking

B–D *(page 131)* Answers will vary.

Video

VIEWING: *VOLCANO TREK* *(page 132)*

Overview of the Video

A research expedition to the Erta Ale volcano in Ethiopia features National Geographic Explorers Dr. Franck Tessier and Dr. Irene Margaritis. Erta Ale is located at one of the lowest points on Earth and houses the oldest lava lake in the world.

BEFORE VIEWING

A **Critical Thinking: Interpreting A Diagram** *(page 132)*

Have students complete the exercise in pairs. Review answers as a class.

Ideas for... CHECKING FOR COMPREHENSION

Ask questions about the diagram, and have students practice using new vocabulary from the unit. For example, ask: What is at the top of a volcano? *(crater)* What comes out of it? *(eruption)* What is underground? *(magma, lava lake)* What is on the side? *(lava)*

B **Prior Knowledge** *(page 133)*

Have a volunteer read the information in the box aloud. If possible, show photos of Dr. Franck Tessier and Dr. Irene Margaritis, as well as any photos of volcanoes the students mention in their discussion.

WHILE VIEWING

C ▶ 1.13 **Understanding Details** *(page 133)*

Have volunteers share with the class how they turned the false sentences into true statements.

D ▶ 1.13 **Critical Thinking: Making Inferences** *(page 133)*

Explain the meaning of *inference* (information that is not given specifically but that we can draw as a logical conclusion from other information that is given). Discuss the answer to the question as a class. Ask students for the evidence they used to support their inference.

AFTER VIEWING

E *(page 133)*

Remind students to write open-ended *wh-* questions to obtain more interesting answers.

F *(page 133)*

Create a list of questions generated by the class on the board.

Ideas for... MULTI-LEVEL CLASSES

Have students do a role-play in mixed-level groups of four. Two students are Dr. Franck Tessier and Dr. Irene Margaritis, and the other two are journalists. Have lower-level students be the journalists and higher-level students be the geologists. The journalists should ask the geologists questions from the list on the board. The geologists should provide answers based on the information from the video.

ANSWER KEY

VIDEO

A *(page 132)* **1.** crater; **2.** magma; **3.** lava; **4.** lava lake; **5.** eruption

B *(page 133)* Answers will vary.

C *(page 133)* **1.** T; **2.** F (They use camels.); **3.** F (They're from the University of Nice.); **4.** T; **5.** F (As lava cools, it becomes black.); **6.** F (The team returns at 2:00 a.m.)

D *(page 133)* Possible answers:

The professors traveled far to see the volcano, and it was difficult to climb, so they must be enthusiastic about their work.

One professor says it is quite exciting.

The professors stay in the crater for a long time. They might not do that if they didn't enjoy the work.

E *(page 133)* Answers will vary.

Lesson B

⏱ 30 MINS VOCABULARY

A 🎧 2.21 **Meaning from Context** *(page 134)*

Have students look at the photo. Read the caption aloud. Give them time to read the facts before listening.

Ideas for... CHECKING FOR COMPREHENSION

Divide the class into groups. Assign one fact to each group. Ask each group to prepare as many questions as they can about their fact that can be answered using the text. With books closed, students can choose a group to answer each question. To make this competitive, you can award points for each question asked and for each correct answer given.

B *(page 135)*

Have students complete the exercise individually and form pairs to compare answers.

C *(page 135)*

Encourage students to use Lesson B vocabulary in their sentences.

Ideas for... PRESENTING THE VOCABULARY SKILL: Using *Affect* and *Effect*

Help students remember the difference between these two similar words with the following trick: Affect with an A is an Action. Effect with an E is an End result.

D **Critical Thinking: Analyzing** *(page 135)*

Have students tear a piece of paper in half and write "A" on one piece and "E" on the other. As a review, read sentences aloud, and ask students to hold up the piece of paper with the first letter of the correct answer.

VOCABULARY

B *(page 135)* **1.** i; **2.** h; **3.** b; **4.** g; **5.** j; **6.** d; **7.** e; **8.** f; **9.** a; **10.** c

C *(page 135)* Possible answers:

1. Volcanic eruptions are dangerous because <u>they can happen without a lot of warning</u>.
2. According to my parents, <u>I do not worry enough about possible disasters</u>.
3. If we ever need to evacuate this building, I'll <u>leave behind almost everything</u>.
4. The worst natural disaster that I remember was <u>the tsunami in the Indian Ocean in 2004</u>.
5. Active volcanoes are <u>unpredictable</u>.
6. <u>Worrying about an earthquake</u> affects my life every day.

D *(page 135)* **1.** affect; **2.** effects; **3.** affects; **4.** effect; **5.** affect; **6.** affect; **7.** effects; **8.** effect

LISTENING: A DISCUSSION ABOUT VOLCANOES

BEFORE LISTENING

A **Predicting** *(page 136)*

Ask volunteers to write their topic ideas on the board. Ask the class which topics they think would be the most interesting to discuss. Have students form pairs and write some questions they have about those topics.

WHILE LISTENING

B 🎧 2.22 **Listening for Main Ideas** *(page 136)*

Have students circle the topics as they hear them.

C 🎧 2.22 **Listening for Details** *(page 136)*

Give students time to review the sentences before listening again.

Ideas for... PRESENTING THE LISTENING SKILL: Listening for Transitions

Read through the information in the box. Have volunteers read the examples aloud. Ask students what they can conclude from each example. For example, in the first example we can conclude that the students will have a total of five assessments this semester: two exams and three quizzes. Ask students to complete each example sentence in a different way, using the same transition; for example, "Living near volcanoes isn't always safe. However, volcanoes bring a lot of tourists to the area."

D 🎧 2.23 **Listening for Transitions** *(page 137)*

Review answers as a class. Have volunteers explain the reasons why the speaker used each particular transition.

AFTER LISTENING

E **Critical Thinking: Reflecting** *(page 137)*

Take a class survey on how many students would like to see a volcano. Have volunteers share reasons why or why not.

LISTENING

A *(page 136)* Answers will vary.

B *(page 136)*

Discussed: a, b, d

Not discussed: c, e

C *(page 136)* **1.** inside; **2.** lava; **3.** start fires; **4.** evacuate; **5.** Fifty-seven (57); **6.** culture

D *(page 137)*

1. addition (In addition,)
2. contrast (On the other hand,)
3. result (As a result,)

E *(page 137)* Answers will vary.

SPEAKING

Ideas for... **PRESENTING PRONUNCIATION:** Syllable Number and Syllable Stress Review

🎧 **2.24** Remind students of the meaning of *syllable* and *syllable stress*. Have them clap or tap out the syllables in the examples as you say the words aloud. Ask volunteers to read the examples of syllable stress aloud. Ask them to exaggerate the pronunciation by making the stressed syllable louder and clearer.

A 🎧 **2.25** *(page 138)*

Have students try to complete the exercise individually first and then compare ideas with partners.

B *(page 138)*

Do the first item as an example. Say either sentence *a* or sentence *b*, and ask students to identify which one you said. Ask students to continue this exercise with partners.

ANSWER KEY

SPEAKING

A *(page 138)*

1. **com**mon (2 syllables)
2. **prac**tical (3 syllables)
3. **cir**cumstances (4 syllables)
4. flow (1 syllable)
5. **sum**marize (3 syllables)
6. clothes (1 syllable)
7. psycho**lo**gical (5 syllables)
8. recom**mend** (3 syllables)
9. rein**force** (3 syllables)
10. **de**finitely (4 syllables)

B *(page 138)* Answers will vary.

FINAL TASK: GIVING A PRESENTATION ABOUT A NATURAL DISASTER

A **Critical Thinking: Evaluating** *(page 139)*

Direct students' attention to the *Everyday Language* box. Review expressions to make guesses. If possible, show different photos of the natural disasters mentioned in the quiz to increase students' understanding.

B **Prior Knowledge** *(page 140)*

Recommend that groups divide up the topics so each group member thinks about just two or three natural disasters. Give them 5 minutes, and then ask them to share their ideas with their group and discuss.

C *(page 140)*

Ask students to take notes on main ideas and important details as they conduct research. Suggest that they download photos or diagrams from the Internet, if some are available.

TIP Some students will need guidance on how to conduct research online or look up information in an encyclopedia. In this case, pair these students with classmate research mentors who are more skilled at doing research. Ask students to help each other. If necessary, provide step-by-step instructions to the class.

D **Organizing Ideas** *(page 140)*

Ask students to not only include facts but also real-life examples in their presentations to make their topic more relevant and to increase the audience's interest.

Ideas for... **PRESENTING THE PRESENTATION SKILL:** Speaking at the Right Pace

Review information in the box. Demonstrate speaking too quickly without pauses and speaking more slowly with pauses. You can do this by reading aloud the information in the box first very quickly and then more slowly. When you have finished, ask students which style they prefer and why. Have them identify appropriate times in the presentation to slow down and pause. If possible, show short videos of presentations, and have students evaluate each speaker's pace.

E **Presenting** *(page 140)*

Set a time limit. Give students time to practice before presenting. Leave time after each presentation for audience members to ask questions or make comments.

ANSWER KEY

FINAL TASK

A *(page 139)* Answers provided on student book page 139.

1. T (up to 300 mph/500 kph); **2.** T; **3.** F (in Chile in 1960); **4.** F (1 in 700,000); **5.** T (Hog Island in 1893); **6.** T; **7.** T (the Peshtigo Fire in 1871); **8.** F (cold liquid raindrops freeze as soon as they touch a surface.)

B–E *(page 140)* Answers will vary.

REFLECTION

- Have students answer questions 1 and 2 on their own, and then discuss their answers in pairs or small groups.
- Ask students to discuss similarities and differences in their answers for questions 1 and 2.
- For question 3, have students compare answers and then write the words about which they are still unsure on the board. Lead a class review of the challenging words, and re-teach terms as necessary.

WONDERS FROM THE PAST

8

ACADEMIC TRACK
Archaeology/Anthropology

ACADEMIC SKILLS

LISTENING	Listening for Examples
	Recording Examples
SPEAKING	Summarizing
	Question Intonation
CRITICAL THINKING	Applying Knowledge

UNIT OVERVIEW

This unit explores interesting facts about historical sites around the world, providing a glimpse into the lifestyle of ancient civilizations that help us not only understand our past but also explain our present.

- **LISTENING A   A Guided Tour of Uxmal:** A tour guide leads a walking tour of the ancient Maya site of Uxmal in Yucatán, Mexico.

- **VIDEO   *Sarah Parcak: Space Archaeologist and Egyptologist*:** National Geographic Explorer Sarah Parcak talks about how she fell in love with archaeology, what a space archaeologist does, and why she believes ancient cultures can help us understand the world we live in today.

- **LISTENING B   A Conversation about an Assignment:** A college student and his professor have a conversation about an oral summary assignment.

For the final task, students draw upon what they have learned in the unit to give an individual presentation about a historical site that interests them.

For additional information about the topics in this unit, here are some suggestions for online search terms: *Easter Island, Moai, San Bartolo murals, Uxmal, Maya civilization, The Seven Wonders of the Ancient World, Giza pyramids, Sarah Parcak, Tutankhamen, Valley of the Kings, Thang Long Imperial Citadel, Great Wall of China*

 UNIT OPENER

THINK AND DISCUSS *(page 141)*

Direct students' attention to the photo, title, and caption. Ask leading questions, such as:
- What is this a statue of? *(an ancient "Moai," more commonly known as an "Easter Island head")*
- Where is it? *(Easter Island)*
- What do you know about it? *(There are more than 900 similar statues on the remote Easter Island, which is in the southeastern Pacific Ocean. It is believed that they were carved from rock sometime between A.D. 1250 and 1500. The average height of the statues is 13 feet, or about 4 meters.)*

ANSWER KEY

THINK AND DISCUSS *(page 141)* Possible answers:

1. Some people believe that the Rapa Nui people constructed the statues to honor their ancestors like gods. Other answer will vary.

2. We will learn about other structures or things that were built or created a long time ago and that we don't know a lot about.

EXPLORE THE THEME *(pages 142–143)*

Have students look at the photos, read the captions, and discuss the questions in small groups. Ask the class "What do you know about these and other ancient civilizations? Are you interested in ancient civilizations? Why or why not?"

ANSWER KEY

EXPLORE THE THEME *(pages 142–143)*

1.–2. Answers will vary.

3. Possible answers: People in ancient Greece had gold. People in ancient Egypt wore beautiful jewelry. The Maya painted their containers. Some of the Maya wore big earrings and hats or crowns. These civilizations valued physical beauty.

4. Answers will vary.

Lesson A

 VOCABULARY

A 🎧 3.2 **Meaning from Context** (page 144)

Have students look at the photos as they read the information before listening. If possible, show a map and point out San Bartolo's exact location.

B (page 145)

Remind students to use context clues to match the words in blue to their definitions. Model and encourage them to practice the pronunciation of new words such as *tomb* (with the silent *b*), *ancient*, *mural*, and *buried*.

C **Critical Thinking: Reflecting** (page 145)

Encourage students to use the new vocabulary in their discussion.

Ideas for... PRESENTING THE VOCABULARY SKILL: Using Antonyms

Review the information and examples in the box. Remind students that a *synonym* is a word that has the same meaning as or a meaning similar to another word. Suggest that students write at least one synonym and antonym every time they learn a new vocabulary word. They can do this in a vocabulary journal or in the textbook.

Ideas for... EXPANSION

Have students work in pairs to come up with antonyms for the following adjectives: *tiny*, *clean*, *complex*, *flat*, *open*, and *special*. Have them use those twelve words to describe the artifacts on pages 142–143.

D (page 145)

Review answers as a class. Challenge students to come up with one more antonym for each underlined word.

LISTENING: A GUIDED TOUR OF UXMAL

45 MINS

BEFORE LISTENING

A **Prior Knowledge** *(page 146)*

Ask students whether they have ever been on a guided tour. Have them share their experiences with the class.

WHILE LISTENING

B 🎧 **3.3** **Listening for Main Ideas** *(page 146)*

Ask volunteers to read the questions aloud. Play the audio while students circle the answers. Go over the answers as a class.

C 🎧 **3.3** **Listening for Details** *(page 147)*

Have students take turns retelling the history of the pyramid in pairs. Give each partner 2 minutes. Have them repeat this activity as many times as possible to increase fluency.

AFTER LISTENING

D *(page 147)*

Brainstorm a few questions with the class. Walk around as students work to help with question formation. Ask each pair of students to write their most interesting question on the board.

E *(page 147)*

Have students choose one member of the group to act as the tour guide. Have the rest of the members ask the tour guide their questions and explain why they are interested.

> **Ideas for... MULTI-LEVEL CLASSES**
>
> Have higher-level students act as the tour guides in exercise E. Ask them to respond based on the information in the listening. Encourage them to be creative in their answers.

ANSWER KEY

LISTENING

A *(page 146)* Possible answers:
1. The ancient Maya people lived in parts of present-day Mexico and Central America, including Guatemala and Belize.
2. The ancient Maya lived in cities such as Palenque, Tikal, Chichen Itza, Uxmal, and Calakmul. They practiced agriculture and had a sophisticated understanding of mathematics and astronomy.

B *(page 146)* **1.** c; **2.** a; **3.** a

C *(page 147)* Possible answers:
1. late Classic period (A.D. 600–900)
2. one night
3. three hundred (300)
4. five (5)
5. the ball court
6. The Jaguar Throne
7. a wild cat, the largest wild cat in the Americas

D–E *(page 147)* Answers will vary.

Ideas for... PRESENTING PRONUNCIATION:
Question Intonation

🎧 **3.4** Review the information, and read the examples aloud. Have students write two more examples for each type of question. Ask them to determine whether the intonation rises or falls in each. Have volunteers read their questions aloud with the correct intonation for the class.

A 🎧 **3.5** *(page 148)*

Play the audio two times. During the first time, ask students to draw the arrows. During the second time, pause after each question while students repeat each question aloud.

B *(page 148)*

Encourage students to ask follow-up questions, when appropriate, to keep the conversation going.

C *(page 148)*

Suggest that students write questions connected to the theme of the lesson (e.g., *Why do people study ancient sites?*).

Ideas for... PRESENTING GRAMMAR FOR SPEAKING: The Passive Voice with the Past

Help students to identify the subject and verb of each example sentence. Ask them to compare the forms of the different examples.

D *(page 149)*

Have a volunteer read the information in the box aloud. Have students complete the exercise individually and then compare answers in pairs.

Ideas for... EXPANSION

Ask students to write three questions about the Seven Wonders of the Ancient World using the passive voice in the past. Have them exchange these questions with partners and research the answers to the new questions they received.

E Critical Thinking: Applying Knowledge
(page 150)

Lead a class discussion as a review. Ask students which of the Seven Wonders of the Ancient World they would most like to have visited and why.

ANSWER KEY

SPEAKING

A *(page 148)*

1. What time are we leaving?
2. Have you ever been to Kazakhstan?
3. How was the walking tour?
4. Did you go there on Friday or Saturday?
5. Is the mural from the early, middle, or late period?
6. Does this story make sense to you?
7. Is the mural in Mexico, Guatemala, or Honduras?
8. Where's the pyramid?

C *(page 148)* Answers will vary.

D *(page 149)* **1.** was built; **2.** were planted; **3.** was constructed; **4.** was destroyed; **5.** was kept; **6.** were needed; **7.** was designed

E *(page 150)*

1. Possible answer: One large statue is the Statue of Liberty, which was a gift from France to the U.S. in the late 1800s. It was built to symbolize American independence and freedom. It was placed on an island in New York Harbor to welcome new immigrants.

2. Possible answer: The Hanging Gardens of Babylon may have been planted because the king loved plants. Similar places today are public gardens and parks. I know that governments protect certain places so that people can enjoy them.

3. Possible answer: Lighthouses are built in order to shine a bright light out to sea and provide ships with important location information. They also warn ships about dangerous land near coastlines.

4. Answers will vary.

LESSON TASK: PRESENTING ANCIENT ARTIFACTS

A **Critical Thinking: Analyzing** *(page 150)*

Have each group member choose one of the three artifacts to read about. Give them 5 minutes to answer the questions. Remind students to use everyday language expressing certainty and uncertainty as they report to their group.

B **Organizing Ideas** *(page 151)*

Have students use their imagination to brainstorm additional details about each artifact.

C *(page 151)*

Remind students to introduce the topic of each segment of their presentation. For example: *I am going to talk about an Anasazi artifact.*

D **Presenting** *(page 151)*

When group discussions are complete, ask the class which artifact they found most interesting and why.

Video

VIEWING: *SARAH PARCAK: SPACE ARCHAEOLOGIST AND EGYPTOLOGIST*

Overview of the Video

National Geographic Explorer Sarah Parcak talks about how she fell in love with archaeology, what a space archaeologist does, and why she believes ancient cultures can help us understand the world we live in today.

BEFORE VIEWING

A *(page 152)*

Have students complete the exercise individually and then form pairs to compare answers.

B *(page 152)*

Take a class survey. Which of these facts did most students already know? Which was the most surprising?

C **Critical Thinking: Making Inferences** *(page 152)*

Ask volunteers to give reasons to explain how they think Sarah Parcak feels about her job.

WHILE VIEWING

D ▶ 1.14 **Understanding Main Ideas** *(page 153)*

Give students time to read through the questions and answer choices before watching the video.

E ▶ 1.14 **Understanding Details** *(page 153)*

Have volunteers share how they corrected the false statements.

AFTER VIEWING

F **Critical Thinking: Reflecting** *(page 153)*

Have students share their questions with the class. Encourage students to make guesses about how Sarah Parcak would answer the questions.

ANSWER KEY

VIDEO

A *(page 152)* **1.** c; **2.** a; **3.** d; **4.** e; **5.** b; **6.** f

B *(page 152)* Answers will vary.

D *(page 153)* **1.** c; **2.** b; **3.** a

E *(page 153)* **1.** T; **2.** T; **3.** F (She uses satellites to map and model ancient civilizations.); **4.** T; **5.** F (She has found more than 3,000 ancient settlements.); **6.** F (There was never a single moment; it's a passion that grew and was nurtured over time.)

F *(page 153)* Answers will vary.

Lesson B

30 MINS VOCABULARY

A 🎧 3.6 **Meaning from Context** *(page 154)*

Ask students to find the past passive verbs in the text. (*was murdered, were scanned*). Have them discuss why the author chose the passive and not the active voice in these cases. (The agent is not known or is not important, and the action is more important than the agent.)

Ideas for... **CHECKING FOR COMPREHENSION**

After listening to and reading the text, ask students to close their books and tell you as much as they can remember about it. Then ask them to open their books and determine whether they were right.

B *(page 155)*

Encourage students to try to remember the words before looking back at the text.

C *(page 155)*

Review answers as a class. Give students time to write five more sentences using the words in blue from exercise A.

D **Critical Thinking: Reflecting** *(page 155)*

Go around the class, and ask each student to share one thing that is precious to him or her and why.

Ideas for... **EXPANSION**

Ask students to discuss the importance of museums and why they are useful. Ask them if they think ancient treasures should be kept in their country of origin or if they should be allowed to go to other countries.

ANSWER KEY

VOCABULARY

B *(page 155)* **1.** treasures; **2.** analyze; **3.** precious; **4.** discovery; **5.** reported; **6.** alive; **7.** ruled; **8.** investigate; **9.** remains; **10.** determined

C *(page 155)* **1.** analyzes; **2.** treasures; **3.** ruled; **4.** report; **5.** discovery

D *(page 155)* Answers will vary.

LISTENING: A CONVERSATION ABOUT AN ASSIGNMENT

BEFORE LISTENING

A *(page 156)*

If possible, show a map, and point out the exact location of Hanoi, Vietnam. Ask comprehension questions about the notes to start the discussion: *What was the documentary about? What was discovered? How was it discovered?*

> **Ideas for... EXPANSION**
>
> Ask students to identify abbreviations and symbols in the notes—*gov't (government), = ("means"), 1,000's (thousands)* and suggest any other words in the notes that could be abbreviated. Then have them rewrite the notes using complete sentences.

WHILE LISTENING

B 🎧 **3.7** **Listening for Main Ideas** *(page 156)*

Give students time to read the questions and answer choices before listening.

> **Ideas for... PRESENTING THE LISTENING SKILL:**
> Listening for Examples
>
> Ask students to define what makes an effective example. Some ideas include using personal experiences, adding details, and using powerful description words.

> **Ideas for... PRESENTING THE NOTE-TAKING SKILL:**
> Recording Examples
>
> Have students read through the information and look at the example abbreviations. Elicit any other abbreviations to record an example, and write student ideas on the board.

C 🎧 **3.7** **Note Taking** *(page 157)*

Play the audio multiple times, if necessary.

AFTER LISTENING

D *(page 157)*

Ask students whether they thought the examples were effective and why.

> **ANSWER KEY**
>
> **LISTENING**
>
> **A** *(page 156)* Answers will vary.
>
> **B** *(page 156)* **1.** a; **2.** c; **3.** b; **4.** b
>
> **C** *(page 157)* Possible answers:
>   1. ex: remains of old buildings (palaces)
>   2. e.g. Who was involved?
>   3. ex: dishes, coins
>
> **D** *(page 157)* Answers will vary.

SPEAKING

Ideas for…**PRESENTING THE SPEAKING SKILL:**
Summarizing

Read through the information in the box. Emphasize
the importance of students using their own words
when summarizing, and point out that synonyms can
be a very useful tool to help them do that.

A 🎧 3.8 **Note Taking** *(page 158)*

Remind students to use abbreviations and symbols
whenever possible.

B **Critical Thinking: Evaluating** *(page 158)*

Have volunteers share their opinions about Silvio's
presentations with the class. Remind them to give
reasons to support their opinions and cite examples from
the presentation.

C **Critical Thinking: Applying** *(page 158)*

Have students discuss which information they included
in the summary with partners.

D **Summarizing** *(page 159)*

Keep time. Give each partner 2 minutes to share his or
her summary.

E **Critical Thinking: Evaluating** *(page 159)*

Encourage students to add any missing information to
their summaries and repeat exercise D.

A *(page 158)* Possible answers:

1. Hanoi, Vietnam
2. in 2002
3. The Vietnamese gov't was constructing a new
   building. They discovered the site when they
   began construction.
4. the Vietnamese government, construction
   workers, and archaeologists
5. They stopped construction and chose a different
   location for the building because the Citadel site
   was important historically.
6. The Citadel became a UNESCO World Heritage
   Site.

B *(page 158)* Answers will vary.

C *(page 158)* Possible answers:

Who discovered the site? (Construction workers)

Where is the site? (Hanoi, Vietnam)

What was found at the site? (palace ruins, coins,
dishes, everyday objects)

How did construction workers know the site
was important? (The government called in
archaeologists to examine the site.)

When was the site found? (2002) When did it
become a UNESCO Heritage Site? (2010)

Why is the site important? (It is important historically
because we can learn a lot about how people lived
in the past from the objects found at the site.)

E *(page 159)* Answers will vary.

FINAL TASK: GIVING A PRESENTATION ABOUT A HISTORICAL SITE

35 MINS

A **Brainstorming** *(page 159)*

Explain that this presentation is a summary of facts based on research, not a summary of an argument, theory, or opinion. Students should not present on a historical site already detailed in this unit.

B **Critical Thinking: Evaluating** *(page 160)*

Suggest students do research online or look up information in an encyclopedia.

> **Ideas for… PRESENTING THE PRESENTATION SKILL:** Using Index Cards
>
> Demonstrate examples of effective and ineffective use of index cards while presenting. Focus on body language, eye contact, and organization. Ask students when and how often they think it's appropriate to look at the cards during the presentation.

C **Organizing Ideas** *(page 160)*

Be sure to check students' index cards before they use them during their presentations. Make sure they are numbered and only include key words and phrases.

D *(page 160)*

Students can also practice their presentations with partners in class.

E **Presenting** *(page 160)*

Have students do peer evaluations according to the questions in exercise E on page 159.

> **ANSWER KEY**
>
> **FINAL TASK**
> **A–E** *(pages 159–160)* Answers will vary.

REFLECTION

- Have students answer questions 1 and 2 on their own, and then discuss their answers in pairs or small groups.
- Ask students to discuss similarities and differences in their answers for questions 1 and 2.
- For question 3, have students compare answers and then write the words about which they are still unsure on the board. Lead a class review of the challenging words, and re-teach terms as necessary.

SPECIES SURVIVAL

ACADEMIC TRACK

Life Science

ACADEMIC SKILLS

LISTENING	Listening for Repeated Words
	Re-Writing Your Notes
SPEAKING	Talking about Causes and Effects
	Stress in Multi-Syllable Words
CRITICAL THINKING	Personalizing

UNIT OVERVIEW

Through the lens of explorers, researchers, and photographers, this unit explores the fascinating ways animal species survive and explains human's impact on species in danger of extinction.

- **LISTENING A** **A Talk about Birds:** A biologist talks about two kinds of finches found in the U.K. and some of their special traits and habits.

- **VIDEO** *Amazing Chameleons:* Learn how and why these charismatic creatures shoot their tongues out like arrows to catch an insect, mimic leaves swaying in the wind, and display their hidden colors.

- **LISTENING B** **A Conversation about a Photo Project:** Friends have a conversation about National Geographic Photographer Joel Sartore's Photo Ark Project. The project began over his concerns about species that are disappearing. Sartore is taking photos of endangered species in human care to raise awareness, and funds.

For the final task, students draw upon what they have learned in the unit to create and present a research proposal.

For additional information about the topics in this unit, here are some suggestions for online search terms: *animal adaptation, Charles Darwin Beagle, human migration, goldfinch and greenfinch, blue wildebeest, Texas horned lizard, dead leaf butterfly, Paul Hebert, DNA bar code, armadillo, Joel Sartore, Photo Ark*

 **UNIT OPENER**

THINK AND DISCUSS *(page 161)*

Direct students' attention to the photo, title, and caption. Ask leading questions, such as:
- What kind of fish is this? *(a lionfish)*
- Why do you think it has this name? *(It looks like it has a big mane, like a lion's.)*

ANSWER KEY

THINK AND DISCUSS *(page 161)*

1. Its color and its poisonous spines keep its enemies away and help it to survive.

2. Possible answer: It means that the unit will discuss the things that help animals to survive in the world and not go extinct.

3. Answers will vary.

EXPLORE THE THEME *(pages 162–163)*

In small groups, have students look at the photos, read the captions, and discuss the questions. Have volunteers share other animal adaptions they know of with the class.

ANSWER KEY

EXPLORE THE THEME *(pages 162–163)*

1. Animals use color to match their surroundings (camouflage), to attract a mate, and to tell predators that they are poisonous.

2. It helps it to reach leaves to eat and to see its predators.

3. Answers will vary.

4. Possible answers: House cats domesticated, or became pets, in order to survive. Now humans protect them. Some animals, such as the pufferfish, can appear larger than they really are to scare away predators.

Lesson A

VOCABULARY
(30 MINS)

A 🎧 3.9 Meaning from Context *(page 164)*

Before reading, ask students whether they've heard of Charles Darwin. Ask "Who is he? What is he known for?" Give students time to read the article before listening to it.

B *(page 164)*

Have students complete the exercise individually and then form pairs to compare answers. Practice the pronunciation of new words such as *diversity*, *identify*, *reproduce*, and *inherit*, focusing on syllable stress.

> **Ideas for… CHECKING COMPREHENSION**
>
> In pairs, have students look at the map and describe the route of the *Beagle*. (On the voyage out, Darwin left England, stopped at the Canary Islands just off the western coast of Africa, and then sailed on to Brazil and around South America, toward Australia. On the voyage home, sailing from the east, the *Beagle* went around the southern tip of Africa, touched Brazil again, and then headed back to England.) Ask them to include important details about what he did on each stop of the trip. Give each partner 3 minutes to describe the trip. Note: H.M.S. means *His* (or *Her*) *Majesty's Ship*.

C 🎧 3.10 *(page 165)*

Have students work in pairs, taking turns reading the text aloud and choosing the correct words. Remind them they may need to change the forms of the words. Review answers as a class.

D Critical Thinking: Analyzing *(page 165)*

Encourage students to use the new vocabulary in their discussion.

ANSWER KEY

VOCABULARY

B *(page 164)* **1.** differed; **2.** identify; **3.** offspring; **4.** diversity; **5.** traits; **6.** reproduce; **7.** adapt; **8.** species; **9.** process; **10.** inherit

C *(page 165)* **1.** diversity; **2.** reproduced; **3.** inherited; **4.** traits; **5.** process

---

D *(page 165)*

1.–2. Answers will vary.

3. Possible answer: Giant pandas are a species of bear that live in China.

4. Answers will vary.

5. Possible answer: Countries with rainforests, like Brazil in South America and Indonesia in Southeast Asia, have a large diversity of plant and animal species.

LISTENING: A TALK ABOUT BIRDS
(45 MINS)

BEFORE LISTENING

A Prior Knowledge *(page 166)*

Have volunteers share any information they know about bird-watching. Ask students to suggest vocabulary related to birds that the biologist may use. Write students' ideas on the board.

WHILE LISTENING

> **Ideas for… PRESENTING THE LISTENING SKILL:**
> Listening for Repeated Words
>
> Review the information in the box. Explain to students that a word family consists of the base form of a word plus its inflected forms (when a word changes its form for a grammatical reason such as including the third person -s, the verbal endings -ed or -ing, etc.) and any derived forms made from affixes, for example, when an ending is added to the word to change its meaning, such as -able, -er, -ish, -less, or -ly.

B 🎧 3.11 ▶ 1.15 Listening for Main Ideas *(page 166)*

Ask students to try to keep track of how many times the speaker says each word as they listen. Have them check each word every time they hear it.

C 🎧 3.11 Listening for Details *(page 167)*

Go over the chart with students, and discuss what information is missing before they listen again.

AFTER LISTENING

D *(page 167)*

Have students compare their notes. Play the audio again, if necessary.

> **Ideas for…PRESENTING THE NOTE-TAKING SKILL:**
> **Re-Writing Your Notes**
>
> It's common for students to take messy and unorganized original notes; however, remind them that it's important that their original notes be clear and comprehensible so they can rewrite them later without any confusion.

E *(page 167)*

Ask students whether it was easy or difficult to re-write their notes and why.

F **Personalizing** *(page 167)*

Have students share the titles of their favorite TV shows or documentary films about nature. Create a recommended viewing list for the class.

ANSWER KEY

LISTENING

A *(page 166)* Answers will vary.

B *(page 166)* All of the words in the box should be checked.

   ✓ Different finches have different traits that help them survive and reproduce. (main idea)

C *(page 167)* Possible answers:

Type of Finch	goldfinch	greenfinch
Where It Lives	UK & other parts of Eur. (N in summer, S in winter)	Most of Europe + NW Africa and Turkey
Special Traits	patch of yellow on wing	large, strong beak
What It Eats	Male: seeds from inside flower Female: other seeds	lg. seeds
Other Habits	Flies to warmer parts of Eur. in winter; Returns to UK in summer	Lives diff. places in diff. seasons. Summer: parks & forests Winter: gardens and farm fields

E *(page 167)* Possible answers:

Where It Lives: The European goldfinch lives in the United Kingdom and other parts of Europe—in northern Europe during the summer, and farther south during the winter. The greenfinch lives in most parts of Europe, and also in northwest Africa and parts of Turkey.

Special Traits: The goldfinch has a patch of bright yellow feathers on each wing. The greenfinch has a large, powerful beak.

What It Eats: The male goldfinch eats the small seeds inside flowers, the female goldfinch eats other small seeds, and the greenfinch eats larger seeds.

Other Habits: Goldfinches fly to warmer parts of Europe in September or October. They return to the United Kingdom in the spring. Greenfinches don't leave in the winter, but they live in different places during different seasons. In the summer, they live in parks and forests. In the winter, they live in people's gardens and in farmers' fields where they can find food.

F *(page 167)* Answers will vary.

SPEAKING

A 🎧 **3.12** *(page 168)*

Play the audio, or read the words aloud. Have students answer the questions together as a class after hearing each word.

> **Ideas for... PRESENTING PRONUNCIATION:**
> Stress in Multi-Syllable Words
>
> 🎧 **3.13** Quickly review the concepts of syllables and stressed syllables. Explain that schwa is the name of the most common reduced vowel sound. Its symbol is /ə/. Play the audio. Ask students to identify the stressed and unstressed syllables by clapping or tapping out the stress pattern of each word. For example, *banana* would be *clap CLAP clap*. Have students pronounce the examples several times.

B 🎧 **3.14** *(page 168)*

Play the audio again so students can hear and repeat the pronunciation.

C 🎧 **3.15** *(page 168)*

Review the information on secondary stress in the *Pronunciation* box before listening. Play the audio again, so students can hear and repeat the pronunciation of *analyze*.

D **Critical Thinking: Analyzing** *(page 168)*

Write one or two names of famous people on the board. Ask students to identify the syllables and the stress patterns of the names. Have them do several more examples in pairs.

> **Ideas for... PRESENTING THE SPEAKING SKILL:**
> Talking about Causes and Effects
>
> Go over the information and examples in the box. Point out that *because, since,* and *due to (the fact that)* are often used to show the relationship between two clauses in the same sentence. *As a result (of this), therefore,* and *consequently* are typically used to show a relationship between two sentences. Point out the punctuation used with *because* and *since*. When the result clause (beginning with *because* or *since*) comes first, it is followed by a comma. When the result clause is second, the comma is not needed. Point out the punctuation with *as a result*. It often comes at the beginning of a sentence and is followed by a comma.

E 🎧 **3.16** *(page 169)*

Review answers as a class.

F *(page 169)*

Remind students to explain natural selection using their own words.

G **Critical Thinking: Analyzing** *(page 170)*

Have partners take turns reading the information aloud. Walk around, and provide help as needed. Have each pair share with the class which behavior was the most surprising or interesting to them and why.

H *(page 171)*

Invite volunteers to read their sentences to the class. Discuss alternative answers.

I **Talking About Causes and Effects** *(page 171)*

Encourage students to show photos of their pets or favorite animals as they discuss them.

SPEAKING

A *(page 168)* **1.** ba-na-na (3 syllables); de-mand (2 syllables); i-den-ti-fy (4 syllables); re-pro-duce (3 syllables) **2.** Bold syllables are stressed. ba-**na**-na; de-**mand**; i-**den**-ti-fy; re-pro-**duce** **3.** banana (2 different vowel sounds, with two schwas /bə'næ-nə/); demand (2 different vowel sounds /də'mænd/); identify (3 different vowel sounds, the same at the beginning and end /aɪ'dɛn-tə-faɪ/); reproduce (3 different vowel sounds = /ri-prə'dus/)

B *(page 168)* **1.** **prac**tical; **2.** com**pare**; **3.** at**tach**ment; **4.** a**vai**lable; **5.** pro**por**tion; **6.** sup**port**

C *(page 168)* **1.** recom**mend**; **2.** **clas**sify; **3.** **at**mosphere; **4.** **quan**tity **5.** ro**man**tic; **6.** disap**pear**

D *(page 168)* Answers will vary.

E *(page 169)*

   2. Because of this **3.** therefore **5.** as a result

G *(page 170)*

1. The blue wildebeest is threatened by lions, leopards, and other predators. The dead leaf butterfly is threatened by birds and other insects. The Texas horned lizard is threatened by snakes, hawks, and coyotes. The opossum is threatened by people, cats, and other predators.

2. The blue wildebeest runs fast. The dead leaf butterfly uses camouflage to avoid being seen. The Texas horned lizard shoots blood from its eyes. The opossum lives in trees, is nocturnal, can play dead, and may even smell bad.

3. Answers will vary.

H *(page 171)* Possible answers:

1. Since lions and leopards eat blue wildebeests, the wildebeests need to run very fast.

2. The butterfly looks like a dead leaf, so predators don't recognize it as food.

3. The lizard can surprise its predators; as a result, the lizard has the chance to escape.

4. The opossum has several survival behaviors. Consequently, it is less likely to be killed or eaten by predators.

5. Because the opossum seems to be dead, predators don't want to eat it.

LESSON TASK: PRESENTING A LIFE LESSON

A **Critical Thinking: Analyzing** *(page 171)*

Have a volunteer read the information in the box aloud. Give students time to answer the question in pairs. Remind them to give reasons and share specific examples as they discuss their answers.

B **Organizing Ideas** *(page 171)*

Share with the class an example of a lesson from your own life to spark discussion and model target language. Allow students to present on a life lesson learned from a friend's or colleague's experience if they prefer.

C **Presenting** *(page 171)*

Read the example aloud. Give students time to practice before they give their presentations.

LESSON TASK

A–C *(page 171)* Answers will vary.

Video

45 MINS **VIEWING: AMAZING CHAMELEONS** *(page 172)*

Overview of the Video

In this video, learn how and why these charismatic creatures shoot their tongues out like arrows to catch an insect, mimic leaves swaying in the wind, and display their hidden colors.

BEFORE VIEWING

A **Meaning from Context** *(page 172)*

Have volunteers take turns reading the *Keys To Chameleon Survival* aloud. Ask students which ability they think is the most interesting or most useful.

B *(page 172)*

Have students complete the exercise individually and then form pairs to compare answers.

WHILE VIEWING

C **▶ 1.16** **Understanding Main Ideas** *(page 173)*

Review answers as a class. Ask volunteers to share how they corrected the false statements.

D **▶ 1.16** **Understanding Details** *(page 173)*

Play the video multiple times, if necessary.

AFTER VIEWING

E **Critical Thinking: Analyzing** *(page 173)*

Have volunteers take turns reading the *Threats To Chameleon Survival* aloud. Make sure students understand the threats before discussing them. Have a volunteer from each group summarize the main points of their discussion for the class.

ANSWER KEY

VIDEO

B *(page 172)* **1.** branches; **2.** rotate; **3.** mimic; **4.** project; **5.** background

C *(page 173)* **1.** T; **2.** F (Females change colors when they are not interested in a male.); **3.** F (Chameleons move in a way that mimics a leaf or branch in the wind.); **4.** T

D *(page 173)* **1.** 202, 42; **2.** 2; **3.** 13; **4.** 36; **5.** 9, 37

E *(page 173)*

1. Changes to habitat, deforestation, and other pressures on habitat are directly related to human activity.

2. Possible answer: They could stop cutting down forests to create farmland and produce less waste.

3. Answers will vary.

Lesson B

⏱ 30 MINS VOCABULARY

A 🎧 **3.17** **Meaning from Context** *(page 174)*

Have students look at the title and predict what the article will be about. Ask them to explain what a bar code is and where you can see one. How does it work? What is it used for?

B *(page 175)*

Ask students whether they know other word forms related to these words such as *gene/genetic, classify/ classification*.

> **Ideas for… EXPANSION**
>
> Have students discuss the pros and cons of using the DNA bar code technique, as opposed to using descriptions to identify and classify different species. Ask "Which technique do you think is better? Why?"

C **Critical Thinking: Analyzing** *(page 175)*

Set a time limit for pair work. Have volunteers share their vocabulary learning techniques with the class.

> **Ideas for… PRESENTING THE VOCABULARY SKILL:**
> Identifying the Correct Definition
>
> As you review the information in the box, either bring up an entry from an online dictionary or show students an entry in a paper dictionary. Have students look up at least two of the vocabulary words in a dictionary and see how many different definitions are provided for each. Then ask them to explain how they were able to identify the correct definitions.

> **Ideas for… EXPANSION**
>
> Have a class discussion and debate on the following topic: What are the pros and cons of using the DNA bar code technique, as opposed to using descriptions to identify and classify different species? Which technique do you think is better? Why?

D *(page 175)*

For question 2, suggest that students look up two or three words and report back to their partner. Ask students whether they were surprised at how many definitions each word had. Why or why not?

> **ANSWER KEY**
>
> **VOCABULARY**
>
> **B** *(page 175)* **1.** aware; **2.** classify; **3.** variations; **4.** technique; **5.** controversial; **6.** sample; **7.** gene; **8.** substances; **9.** sequences; **10.** argued
>
> **C** *(page 175)* **1.–3.** Answers will vary.
>
>   **4.** People can organize educational events or throw animal-themed parties.
>
> **D** *(page 175)*
>
>   **1.** definition 1
>
>   **2.** Answers will vary, but students should find more than one definition for each word.

LISTENING: A CONVERSATION ABOUT A PHOTO PROJECT

BEFORE LISTENING

A Prior Knowledge *(page 176)*

Have a volunteer read the information about Joel Sartore aloud. Have students share the names of species they know have gone extinct or endangered species they know and care about. Write students' ideas on the board.

WHILE LISTENING

B ∩ 3.18 Listening for Main Ideas *(page 176)*

Ask volunteers to share how they corrected the false statements.

C ∩ 3.18 Listening for Details *(page 177)*

Give students time to read the questions before they listen to the interview again.

AFTER LISTENING

D Personalizing *(page 177)*

Invite a volunteer from the class to lead a class discussion for question 3. Come up with a class list of tips to help protect endangered species that the students themselves can follow.

> **Ideas for… MULTI-LEVEL CLASSES**
>
> Based on the ideas from the class brainstorming session, have lower-level students make a "how to" pamphlet of products and foods to avoid, as well as actions that can be taken to help endangered species. Higher-level students could write a letter to the editor about their concern regarding the extinction of animal species. Remind them to include expressions to describe cause and effect in their letter.

> **Ideas for… PRESENTING GRAMMAR FOR SPEAKING:** Phrasal Verbs
>
> Review the information in the box. Read through the examples and point out why the phrasal verbs are transitive or intransitive and separable or inseparable. Demonstrate that phrasal verbs have their own nonliteral meanings with the example *look up.* Mime the action of looking up (at the sky) to show the literal meaning and looking up a word in the dictionary to show the nonliteral meaning. Ask students how both of these meanings are different from the stand-alone verb *look.*

A ∩ 3.19 *(page 178)*

Before listening, give students time to read the phone conversation. Afterward, ask them to cover the text and answer a few comprehension questions. For example, ask "Why did Matt decide to go on the expedition? What did Matt almost do?"

B *(page 179)*

Encourage students to think about the literal meaning of each verb + particle, as well as the meaning of the phrasal verb. Then remind them to look at context clues to help them choose the best definition. Tell students to check the meanings of these phrasal verbs in the dictionary. Ask "What other information does the dictionary give about these verbs?"

C *(page 179)*

Have volunteers role-play the conversation for the class.

D *(page 179)*

Review answers as a class. Go over the information in the *Everyday Language* box. Point out that appropriate and enthusiastic intonation is important to make these expressions sound sincere.

ANSWER KEY

LISTENING

A *(page 176)* Answers will vary.

B *(page 176)* **1.** F (He wants to photograph all of the species that are in human care.); **2.** T; **3.** F (It shows images of animals in zoos or in captivity.); **4.** T

C *(page 177)* **1.** Y; **2.** N; **3.** Y; **4.** Y

D *(page 177)* Answers will vary.

Ideas for... EXPANSION

Have students brainstorm examples of things they have done recently about which they are excited; for example, *I rode my bike for 10 miles.* Then have them take turns with partners sharing exciting news or accomplishments and giving congratulations.

FINAL TASK: PRESENTING A RESEARCH PROPOSAL

A *(pages 179–180)*

Conduct a class brainstorming session on different areas of scientific interest related to animals, such as birds, reptiles, insects, mammals, and fish. Put students in groups of three. Give them time to work on the proposal.

Ideas for... PRESENTING THE PRESENTATION SKILL: Timing Your Presentation

Have students share ideas about how they time themselves (e.g., on their cell phone, on a website, on a stopwatch).

B **Organizing Ideas** *(page 180)*

Be sure each group member has a role and is participating.

C **Presenting** *(page 180)*

Encourage audience members to congratulate each group after their presentation.

REFLECTION

- Have students answer questions 1 and 2 on their own, and then discuss their answers in pairs or small groups.
- Ask students to discuss similarities and differences in their answers for questions 1 and 2.
- For question 3, have students compare answers and then write the words about which they are still unsure on the board. Lead a class review of the challenging words, and re-teach terms as necessary.

ENTREPRENEURS AND INNOVATORS

10

ACADEMIC TRACK
Business

ACADEMIC SKILLS
LISTENING	Distinguishing Facts and Opinions
	Reviewing and Editing Your Notes
SPEAKING	Rephrasing
	Thought Groups
CRITICAL THINKING	Interpreting Data

UNIT OVERVIEW

This unit explores the characteristics, motivations, and visions of successful entrepreneurs and innovators within a global landscape that increasingly demands creative solutions to solve contemporary social problems.

- **LISTENING A A Presentation about a Success Story:** A business conference presentation about Howard Schultz and the story of Starbucks.

- **VIDEO *Eco-Fuel Africa:*** Social entrepreneur and National Geographic Explorer Sanga Moses explains his inspiration for providing Africa with clean and inexpensive cooking fuel and how this not only helps the environment, but also empowers his fellow Africans who play an important role in his innovative business.

- **LISTENING B A Conversation about Jack Andraka:** Students have a conversation about National Geographic Explorer Jack Andraka who invented a new test for pancreatic, ovarian, and lung cancer.

For the final task, students draw upon what they have learned in the unit to participate in a role-play about a new product or service that they present to investors.

For additional information about the topics in this unit, here are some suggestions for online search terms: *Mitsunobu Okada, ADRASI, Arturo Vittori, WarkaWater, Charlie Harry, edible mist machine, Archel Bernard, Kieran and Sean Murphy, Howard Schultz, Detroit Michigan, Sanga Moses, Eco-Fuel Africa, Chandra Shroff, Kutch Gujarat India, Jack Andraka, Edwin Van Ruymbeke, Bionic Bird drone*

UNIT OPENER

THINK AND DISCUSS *(page 181)*

Direct students' attention to the photo, title, and caption. Ask leading questions, such as:
- Who is this man? *(Mitsunobu Okada)*
- What is he holding? *(a model of the satellite ADRASI)*
- Where does he work? *(a start-up company called Astroscale)*

> ### ANSWER KEY
>
> **THINK AND DISCUSS** *(page 181)*
>
> Possible answers:
> 1. It cleans up trash in space.
> 2. Entrepreneurs are people who start a new business or enterprise. Innovators are people who create new things or come up with new ways of doing things.

EXPLORE THE THEME *(pages 182–183)*

In small groups, have students look at the photos, read the captions, and discuss the questions. Pronounce the words *entrepreneur* (on-truh-pruh-NUR) and *entrepreneurial* (on-truh-pruh-NUR-ee-uhl), and have students repeat. Ask students what words or phrases they associate with *entrepreneur* and *innovator*. Write students' ideas on the board. Ask students to describe someone they know or have heard of who has started his or her own business.

> Ideas for… **EXPANSION**
>
> Have students form pairs and make a chart that lists the advantages and disadvantages of working for a company and working for yourself. Ask volunteers to write their ideas in a chart on the board. Lead a class discussion.

> ### ANSWER KEY
>
> **EXPLORE THE THEME** *(pages 182–183)*
>
> 1. Possible answers: creative, hard-working, confident, optimistic, persistent, etc.
> 2. Answers will vary.
> 3. Possible answers: The water tower is probably the most useful because clean water is so important. The machine that allows you to inhale tastes is fun, but less useful.
> 4. Answers will vary.

Lesson A

🕐 **30 MINS** **VOCABULARY**

A 🎧 **1.18** **Meaning from Context** *(page 184)*

Put students in groups of three. Have them take turns reading each of the six common traits aloud before listening.

Ideas for... EXPANSION

Ask students to do a 3-minute free writing exercise in which they answer the following questions: Do you think you have what it takes to be a successful entrepreneur? Why or why not? Then have them share their ideas in pairs.

B *(pages 184–185)*

Ask students to underline the vocabulary word in each sentence. Have them complete the exercise individually. Review answers as a class. Have volunteers explain how they corrected the false statements.

Ideas for... MULTI-LEVEL CLASSES

To make this exercise more challenging, ask students to think of other words related to each word in blue; for example: *motivation* ⟶ *motivational, motivating.*

C **Critical Thinking: Reflecting** *(page 185)*

Tell students to use examples from their personal experience to support their statements.

Ideas for... PRESENTING THE VOCABULARY SKILL: Recognizing Adjectives and Adverbs

Elicit additional examples of adjectives with the suffixes listed in the box. Write students' ideas on the board. Lead a word association activity with the class. Say one of the adjectives listed on the board, and have a student call out a noun associated with it. For example, you may say, "famous," and a student may respond with "celebrities!"

D *(page 185)*

Review answers as a class. Have students give reasons to explain the correct answer choices.

ANSWER KEY

VOCABULARY

B *(page 184)* **1.** T; **2.** T; **3.** T; **4.** F (Failures are when things go badly and you don't get what you want.); **5.** F (They happen after some time.); **6.** T; **7.** F (It changes over time.); **8.** T; **9.** F (If something is essential, you really need it.); **10.** T

C *(page 185)* Answers will vary.

D *(page 185)* **1.** permanent, regional; **2.** well, confident; **3.** persistent, ideal; **4.** capable, independently, eventually; **5.** perfect, highly, good

LISTENING: A PRESENTATION ABOUT A SUCCESS STORY

BEFORE LISTENING

A Prior Knowledge *(page 186)*

Have students share their ideas and opinions with the class. If possible, bring up a company's logo or website as they describe what makes it so successful. Show images of two brands of the same product side by side, and have students explain which they would rather buy and why.

WHILE LISTENING

B 🎧 3.21 ▶ 1.17 Listening for Main Ideas
(page 186)

Ask students whether they've ever heard of Howard Schultz. Ask them what they know about the company Starbucks. Give students time to read the sentences before listening. Review answers as a class.

> **Ideas for... PRESENTING THE LISTENING SKILL:**
> **Distinguishing Facts and Opinions**
>
> Review the information in the box. Ask students how they know whether a source of information is reliable. Ask students to write three facts and three opinions about a certain topic with which they are all familiar (e.g., the school, a nearby restaurant, a well-known figure). Have volunteers share their sentences with the class. Ask the class "Do you agree that this is a fact?" or "Do you agree that this is an opinion? Why or why not?"

TIP When students are researching facts, advise them to consider the following questions to determine whether a source is reliable:
- Is there an author? *(Be aware of sources where anyone can add or change content.)*
- Who is the author? *(Credible sources are written by respected authors who cite their sources.)*
- How recent is the source? *(Depending on the topic, sources should provide up-to-date information.)*
- What is the author's purpose? *(Don't limit research to just one perspective or side of a debate.)*
- Who paid for the research or publication? *(Look for funding information and research the background.)*
- Has the source been reviewed by others? *(If the source is academic, it should be peer reviewed.)*

C 🎧 3.21 Listening for Details *(page 187)*

Give students time to read the sentences before listening. Have them predict which words will fill in each blank.

D *(page 187)*

Have volunteers share their answers and give reasons to explain their choices.

> **Ideas for... EXPANSION**
>
> Have students form pairs to read news headlines online or in a newspaper and discuss whether what they read is fact or opinion. Ask "How do you know?"

AFTER LISTENING

E Critical Thinking: Analyzing *(page 187)*

To help students complete the exercise from a business point of view, suggest they imagine they are the CEO of their favorite company. How would he or she respond to each statement?

> **ANSWER KEY**
>
> **LISTENING**
>
> **A** *(page 186)* Answers will vary.
>
> **B** *(page 186)* **1.** Y; **2.** Y; **3.** N; **4.** Y; **5.** Y; **6.** N
>
> **C** *(page 187)* **1.** the company; **2.** it seems; **3.** ask me; **4.** receive stock; **5.** how great; **6.** in 2000
>
> **D** *(page 187)* **1.** fact (verbs "isn't" and "did start"); **2.** opinion (use of "it seems"); **3.** opinion (use of "if you ask me"); **4.** fact (verbs "are" and "can receive"); **5.** opinion (adjective implies opinion); **6.** fact (verb phrase "was in 2000" is fact)
>
> **E** *(page 186)* Answers will vary.

Ideas for… **PRESENTING GRAMMAR FOR SPEAKING:** The Present Perfect And Signal Words

Read the information in the box, and have volunteers read the example sentence aloud. Review the meanings of the signal words in context. Invite volunteers up to the board to draw timelines of the sentences and explain the meaning of the present perfect in each case by referring back to the explanations in the box. They should also explain what information the signal word adds to the sentence.

A *(page 188)*

Have students work individually and then form pairs to compare their answers. Walk around, and provide help as needed. If necessary, hand out a list of irregular past participles for reference.

B *(page 189)*

Ask students to continue asking and answering present perfect questions using their own ideas.

Ideas for… **EXPANSION**

Have students make a list of interesting activities they have done or would like to do. Ask them to stand up and ask different classmates whether they have done any of these activities. The exercise should continue until students have talked to each of their classmates at least once.

Ideas for… **PRESENTING PRONUNCIATION:** Thought Groups

🎧 3.22 Review the information in the box. Explain to students that the pause between thought groups is very short. Read the example sentences aloud with both appropriate and exaggerated pauses. Ask students which they think sounds best and why. Ask which sounds more natural.

C 🎧 3.23 *(page 189)*

Answer question 1 as a class. As a review, write the sentences on the board, and have volunteers put the slashes in the correct places.

Ideas for… **PRESENTING THE SPEAKING SKILL:** Rephrasing

Have volunteers read the conversation in the box aloud. Ask the class exactly which parts of speaker A's sentences were rephrased and how. (*I haven't seen* ➔ *since I saw*; *Masayo* ➔ *your brother*; *in ages* ➔ *It's been a long time*) Have students come up with a short list of ways to rephrase ideas. For example:

1. Change word form (e.g., change verb tense, such as *I haven't seen* ➔ *since I saw*).

2. Change word order (e.g., break up long thoughts, combine short thoughts, add details for clarity).

3. Be more specific or more general (e.g., change proper nouns to common nouns, such as *Masayo* ➔ *your brother*).

4. Use synonyms or a phrase that expresses the same meaning (e.g., *in ages* ➔ *It's been a long time*).

D **Rephrasing** *(page 190)*

Remind students to use the expressions for rephrasing from the *Speaking Skill* box in their answers.

E *(page 190)*

Encourage students to underline any words they don't know. Review new vocabulary with the class.

F **Rephrasing** *(page 191)*

Have two volunteers retell Part A and Part B for the class.

G **Personalizing** *(page 191)*

Remind students to share their personal opinions and experiences. Lead a class discussion about cities around the world that are thriving economically and what kinds of jobs are available there.

ANSWER KEY

SPEAKING

A *(page 188)* **1.** has been; **2.** have called, haven't answered; **3.** Have you ever stayed; **4.** has always wanted; **5.** have owned; **6.** have bought, has been, has never been; **7.** has worked; **8.** haven't sent

B *(page 189)*

Questions:

1. Have you ever taken a class in business or economics?

2. Have you ever bought a coffee drink at Starbucks?

3. Have you ever visited your country's capital city?

4. Have you ever gotten paid for your work?

5. Have you ever been interviewed for a job?

6. Have you ever thought about starting your own company?

   Answers to questions will vary.

C *(page 189)*

1. My best friend started her own company/about five years ago/right after college.

2. Her son wants to study business/and then work at a bank.

3. Running a successful business is not easy/because you work a lot/and have to take risks.

4. I got a job/at the new café/on Main Street.

5. If you work hard/and treat people well/you'll be successful.

6. After work/I usually take a walk/so I can relax/and get some exercise.

D *(page 190)* Possible answers:

1. In other words, I'm hungry.

2. What I mean is, why did you decide to study English?

3. In other words, our English teacher is a real grammar expert.

4. That is, I want to be an entrepreneur.

5. To clarify, do you believe in yourself and your abilities?

6. In other words, I've never bought anything online.

G *(page 191)* Answers will vary.

LESSON TASK: INTERPRETING QUOTATIONS

A **Critical Thinking: Interpreting Quotations** *(page 191)*

As a review, write each quote down on a piece of paper. Invite six volunteers up to the front of the classroom. Have them choose a piece of paper and rephrase the quote in front of the class. After each quote, take a class survey on who agrees and disagrees. Have a spokesperson from each side give reasons to explain why.

B **Critical Thinking: Reflecting** *(page 191)*

Encourage students to choose entrepreneurs and innovators from their home country or countries.

ANSWER KEY

LESSON TASK

A–B *(page 191)* Answers will vary.

Video

VIEWING: *ECO-FUEL AFRICA*
(page 192)

Overview of the Video

Social entrepreneur and National Geographic Explorer Sanga Moses explains his inspiration for providing Africa with clean and inexpensive cooking fuel and how this not only helps the environment, but also empowers his fellow Africans who play an important role in his innovative business.

BEFORE VIEWING

A *(page 192)*

Have a volunteer read the information about Sanga Moses in the box aloud. Have students form pairs, and have each pair make a chart to show how social entrepreneurs differ from other entrepreneurs. (Entrepreneurs have innovative solutions to existing problems. Social entrepreneurs have innovative solutions specifically to society's most pressing social problems.) As a review, write students' ideas on the board.

B Personalizing *(page 192)*

Have pairs join to make groups of four. Encourage students to share their childhood experiences. Ask the class which group members have similar backgrounds and how they think their backgrounds shaped who they are today.

WHILE VIEWING

C ▶ 1.18 **Understanding Main Ideas** *(page 193)*

Give students time to read the statements and possible answers before watching.

D ▶ 1.18 **Understanding Details** *(page 193)*

Play the video again. If necessary, pause after each number to give students time to fill in the blanks.

AFTER VIEWING

E Critical Thinking: Interpreting Data *(page 193)*

Read the information in the *Critical Thinking* box. Ask students in what situation they might have to interpret data in their own lives. Have a volunteer read aloud the data about Uganda in the box. Check students' understanding of the data. Ask "What information do these data provide? How are these data important or relevant to the topic or situation?" Have volunteers share their ideas and answers to the questions with the class.

ANSWER KEY

VIDEO

A–B *(page 192)* Answers will vary.

C *(page 193)* **1.** sister; **2.** shocked; **3.** furniture; **4.** CEO; **5.** follow

D *(page 193)* **1.** 2; **2.** 65; **3.** 105,000; **4.** 10, 16

E *(page 193)*

1. Answers will vary.
2. Possible answers: The literacy rate for girls is lower. This information supports Moses's concern that girls have to take time away from school to find and carry wood for cooking.
3. Answers will vary.

Lesson B

VOCABULARY
30 MINS

A 🎧 3.24 *(page 194)*

Ask students what they know about the economy in India. Have them describe what and who they see in the photo. Give them time to read the information before listening.

B *(page 194)*

Remind students to use parts of speech and context clues to match the words in blue to their meanings. Have students compare these definitions with those in a dictionary and find additional meanings for these words.

C *(page 195)*

Encourage students to use their general knowledge, as well as the information in the text, to answer these questions. Have volunteers share how they corrected the false statements.

D **Critical Thinking: Analyzing** *(page 195)*

Remind students to use expressions for rephrasing in question 1 and provide reasons for their opinions in question 2.

ANSWER KEY

VOCABULARY

B *(page 194)* **1.** probability; **2.** achieve; **3.** recognition; **4.** potential; **5.** income; **6.** evidently; **7.** appreciate; **8.** founded; **9.** considerable; **10.** mission

C *(page 195)* **1.** T; **2.** F (If a company earns considerable profits, it is making a lot of money.); **3.** F (Someone who founded a company started it.); **4.** F (Investors will probably lend you money if your company has the potential to succeed.); **5.** T

D *(page 195)* Answers will vary.

 LISTENING: A CONVERSATION ABOUT JACK ANDRAKA
45 MINS

BEFORE LISTENING

A *(page 196)*

Have a volunteer read the information in the box aloud. Give students time to discuss the questions in pairs. Ask the class who has a strong motivation to solve a problem, and invite that student to share his or her story with the class. Have the students think of some possible solutions for their classmate's problem.

WHILE LISTENING

B 🎧 3.25 **Listening for Main Ideas** *(page 197)*

Give students time to read through the partial notes so they know what information to listen for.

C 🎧 3.25 **Listening for Details** *(page 197)*

Play the audio as many times as necessary for students to complete their notes.

AFTER LISTENING

> **Ideas for… PRESENTING THE NOTE-TAKING SKILL:**
> **Reviewing And Editing Your Notes**
>
> Have students share their note-taking preferences. For example, do they like to use highlighters? How do they mark key ideas and important details? Which organization format works best for each of them? Encourage students to try their classmates' strategies.

D *(page 197)*

Walk around, and provide help as needed.

E *(page 197)*

Have each student retell Jack Andraka's story to a partner to review and summarize the information in his or her notes.

F Critical Thinking: Ranking *(page 197)*

Remind students to give reasons to support their opinions.

G *(page 197)*

Do a class ranking of the factors on the board. Allow students to try to persuade each other to change their rankings with good reasons.

ANSWER KEY

LISTENING

A *(page 196)* Answers will vary.

B *(page 197)* Possible answers:

Jack Andraka's mission: find a better, cheaper test for cancer

If Dr.s detect cancer early → higher probability treated and survive

Andraka's test: 1. cheap (costs 3 cents) 2. fast (takes 5 minutes) 3. better than existing test; existing test = expensive + not accurate

Test not available yet (still needs more testing)

C *(page 197)* Possible answers:

Jack Andraka's mission: find a better, cheaper test for cancer

-a good family friend died of pancreatic cancer

If Dr.s detect cancer early → higher probability treated and survive

Andraka's test: 1. cheap (costs 3 cents) 2. fast (takes 5 minutes)

-special piece of paper; Andraka has gotten a lot of recognition for the test

3. better than existing test; existing test = expensive + not accurate

-It doesn't detect cancer early enough

Test not available yet (still needs more testing)

-Need to be sure test works; it has the potential to save lives

F *(page 197)* Answers will vary.

SPEAKING

> **Ideas for… PRESENTING GRAMMAR FOR SPEAKING: Infinitives to Show Purpose**
>
> Remind students that an infinitive is the word *to* plus the base form of a verb. Give examples (*to study, to write, to make, to think*, etc.) Review the information and examples in the box. Explain to students that both *in order to* and *to* have the same meaning and express the same level of purpose. They can use whichever expression they prefer. Ask students to explain the function of the infinitives in the example sentences. For example, *in order to start* in the first example explains why Elias borrowed a lot of money.

A *(page 198)*

Give students time to brainstorm answers individually before working in pairs.

B *(page 198)*

Have students work with different partners than the ones they had for exercise A.

SPEAKING

A *(page 198)* Possible answers:

1. Howard Schultz chooses to pay employees a little more to make their lives better.

2. Starbucks partners write the customer's name on the coffee cup to make the customers feel like individuals or friends.

3. Chanda Shroff commissioned 30 saris from Kutch women to sell at an art exhibit.

4. Shroff founded the Shrujan organization to help Kutch women earn an income.

5. Jack Andraka invented a new cancer test to help doctors detect cancer in its early stages.

6. The test uses a special kind of paper to detect cancer.

7. Many people become doctors in order to help people.

8. People go to business school to learn how to manage a business.

9. We are meeting with potential investors in order to develop a relationship with them.

10. The company hired ten new sales people to increase their sales revenue.

B *(page 198)* Possible answers:

1. People take test preparation courses to (in order to) improve their test scores.

2. People spend time with their friends to (in order to) relax and have fun.

3. Businesses have to advertise to (in order to) sell their products.

4. People drink coffee or tea in the morning to (in order to) feel awake.

5. People go to the library to (in order to) do research.

6. I take notes in class to (in order to) remember important information.

7. I'm learning English to (in order to) get a better job.

8. I use the Internet to (in order to) access information.

9. I use a weather app to (in order to) check the forecast.

10. People visit New York to (in order to) see the Statue of Liberty.

FINAL TASK: PRESENTING A NEW PRODUCT

A Brainstorming *(page 199)*

Read the assignment aloud for the class. Explain the role of an investor in a new business. (Investors provide funds in exchange for an ownership stake in the company or future return of profit.) Lead a class discussion. Write students' ideas on the board for reference.

B Organizing Ideas *(page 200)*

Make sure each pair of students is presenting on a different product or service. Encourage students to be realistic and specific in their business proposals.

> **Ideas for… PRESENTING THE PRESENTATION SKILL:** Thinking about Your Audience
>
> Have students answer the example questions for an audience of potential investors. Review these answers as a class, and write students' ideas on the board.

C *(page 200)*

Encourage students to videotape their practice presentations and analyze their verbal and nonverbal communication before they give their presentations.

D Presenting *(page 200)*

Remind students to give each other specific reasons and feedback from an investor's point of view. Encourage them to use the expressions for complimenting someone listed in the *Everyday Language* box on page 199.

FINAL TASK

A–D *(pages 199–200)* Answers will vary.

REFLECTION

- Have students answer questions 1 and 2 on their own, and then discuss their answers in pairs or small groups.
- Ask students to discuss similarities and differences in their answers for questions 1 and 2.
- For question 3, have students compare answers and then write the words about which they are still unsure on the board. Lead a class review of the challenging words, and re-teach terms as necessary.

AUDIO SCRIPTS

CD1

Unit 1: Healthy Lives

LESSON A   Vocabulary

Track 1.2   B.   Page 4

How old is the oldest person you know? Eighty years old? Ninety years old? In some parts of the world, it's not unusual for people to live 100 years or even longer.

Researchers looked at two of these places—Sardinia, Italy, and Okinawa, Japan—and learned that people there suffer from fewer diseases than in other parts of the world. They're also more likely to live to be 100 or older.

In Sardinia, researchers were surprised to find as many men as women who were 100 years old or older. This is unusual because in general, women live longer than men. One reason for this may be that men in Sardinia don't have a lot of stress in their lives, and stress can cause high blood pressure. The men there work outdoors, which provides daily exercise, while the women take care of the house and money. According to one Sardinian man, he does the work, but his wife does the worrying.

In Okinawa, people have very low rates of cancer and heart disease. One of the reasons could be their positive attitude toward life, which may prevent stress. Okinawans also eat a healthy diet that consists of a lot of fresh vegetables and a little meat and fish. Along with healthy habits, such as gardening and spending time with family, a positive attitude and good food seem to prevent many of the health problems found in other parts of the world.

Listening: A Talk about Preventing Heart Disease

Track 1.3   A.   Page 6

Tara: Hello, everyone, and thanks for coming. I'd like to introduce myself. I'm Tara Sorenson, and I'm a public health nurse. Public health nurses are like other nurses, but we take care of more than one person. Our job is to keep everyone in the community healthy. I know—it's a *big* job! Mostly, I do this through education. Tonight, I'm going to talk with you about heart disease and how to prevent it. I'm hoping to provide information that will help all of you to live longer, healthier lives.

Track 1.4   C. Checking Predictions,   Page 6
D. Listening for Main Ideas, and   Page 7
E. Listening for Details

Tara: Hello, everyone, and thanks for coming. I'd like to introduce myself. I'm Tara Sorenson, and I'm a public health nurse. Public health nurses are like other nurses, but we take care of more than one person. Our job is to keep everyone in the community healthy. I know—it's a *big* job! Mostly, I do this through education. Tonight, I'm going to talk with you about heart disease and how to prevent it. I'm hoping to provide information that will help all of you to live longer, healthier lives.

OK, many people in this country suffer from heart disease, and maybe you know someone who does, or you're worried about developing heart disease yourself. The good news is—there are several things you can do to *prevent* it! The first thing is pretty easy—get your blood pressure checked. High blood pressure is a serious problem, and it can lead to heart disease. So if you *do* have high blood pressure, you need to do something about it. For example, if you're overweight, losing five or ten pounds could help lower your blood pressure. Or you might need to take medication if your blood pressure is quite high. It's really important to watch your blood pressure, so remember to get it checked.

Let's talk about diet next. Now—I'm not talking about a special diet where you eat only apples and lemons for a week—nothing like that! I'm talking about healthy eating habits—how you eat most of the time. According to government reports, a healthy diet can keep your weight and your blood pressure down, and it can help prevent heart disease. For example, you should eat several servings of vegetables and fruits every day and eat less salt and sugar. You should also choose low-fat dairy products such as low-fat milk and yogurt and eat healthy protein foods like fish and chicken and only small amounts of red meat.

These are things you can do every day—or at least most of the time. I know—nobody is perfect, right? Furthermore, these healthy eating habits can help control your blood *sugar*. This is important because high blood sugar can also cause heart disease. A lot of people don't realize this.

Besides high blood pressure and high blood sugar, another common cause of heart disease is smoking. I guess everyone knows it's a very *un*healthy habit, so if you want to prevent heart disease, you *have* to quit smoking.

Well, now let's talk about *exercise* as a way to prevent heart disease. I recommend exercising at least four or five times a week, for at least 30 minutes. You can walk, or run, or play a sport—any activity that you enjoy. *Regular exercise* will make your heart stronger and make you healthier. And it can be fun, too!

Another way to prevent heart disease is to find healthy ways to deal with stress. After all, our daily lives consist of jobs and children and other things that keep us very busy and can contribute to stress. So, when you feel stressed out, go for a walk or practice yoga! Then make a healthy dinner for your family and get a good night's sleep. If you do these things, you will probably find that you have a better attitude right away and feel more relaxed, *and* you'll be much less likely to suffer from heart disease in the future. Of course, it's also important to visit your doctor regularly.

All right. To sum up, preventing heart disease is one of the *best* things you can do for yourself. So, remember to get your blood pressure checked, since high blood pressure can contribute to heart disease. Eat a healthy diet, and remember that high blood *sugar* is as much of a problem for your heart as high blood *pressure*. If you smoke, quit. I don't need to explain that one. Exercise regularly. This will help prevent heart disease along with *several* other health problems. And finally, find healthy ways to deal with stress. If you do these things, chances are you won't suffer from heart disease and you'll live a longer healthier life. Well, I hope this advice is helpful to you. Now, are there any questions? Yes, the man in the back.

Speaking

Track 1.5   Pronunciation: Final -s
Sounds   Page 8

hour → hours   like → likes   provide → provides
habit → habits   bus → buses   wash → washes
exercise → exercises

Track 1.6   A.   Page 8

1. Frank exercises every day. He plays sports and lifts weights.
2. There are 16 doctors and 37 nurses at the hospital.
3. I eat pears, peaches, and other kinds of fruit almost every day.
4. Stress causes a lot of health problems.
5. The yoga class begins when the teacher closes the door.

Lesson Task: Presenting Healthy Habits

Track 1.7   A.   Page 11

Hello, my name is Adriana Santos.

To stay healthy, I exercise—but not every day. I usually exercise four or five days a week. I also take vitamins every day.

For exercise, I usually jog two or three times a week. I also walk. I live nearby, so I walk to class every day, actually. Sometimes I go biking, but I don't have my own bike, so I can ride only on weekends in the park. They rent bikes in the park on Saturdays and Sundays.

In the future, I want to have a healthier diet. Now, I live in a very small apartment with no kitchen. I eat a lot of fast food because I can't cook for myself. After I graduate, I plan to move to a bigger apartment with a kitchen. I also want to get my own bike so I can bike every day.

Staying healthy is very important to me. If I do all of these things now, maybe I'll live to be 100! Thank you very much.

LESSON B   Vocabulary

Track 1.8   A. Meaning from Context   Page 14

Allergies

What are allergies? If you have an *allergy* to something, you become sick, or have an *allergic reaction*, when you eat, smell, or touch it. Many people are allergic to pollen. The diagram below shows what happens when there is an allergic reaction to pollen.

1. First, pollen enters the body through the nose or mouth.
2. Second, the body's immune system responds to the pollen with IgE antibodies. These antibodies attach to a mast cell. A mast cell is a cell that usually defends your body against health problems.
3. The next time the same pollen enters the body, the IgE antibodies "tell" the mast cell. The mast cell "thinks" there is a problem and tries to defend the body.
4. When this occurs, the mast cell produces substances in the body that cause allergic reactions such as sneezing, itching, and breathing problems.

Track 1.9   C. Meaning from Context   Page 15

Allergies and the Hygiene Hypothesis

Many people work very hard to keep their houses clean. But can too much cleanliness cause health problems? One theory is that dirt is good for us. Dirt on farms, for example, contains substances that exercise our immune systems when we're very young. Research shows that allergies are not common among people who live with farm animals. Of course, there are many causes of allergies. For example, if your parents have allergies, you're more likely to have them, too. The stress of modern life could be another cause. But if the hygiene hypothesis is correct, it might be a good idea to have a cow at your house—or at least not to worry so much about cleanliness.

Listening: A Conversation about Allergies

Track 1.10   B. Listening for Main Ideas and   Page 16
C. Note Taking

Raymond: Hey, Elena – How's it going?

Elena: I'm fine, thanks. I saw you in Professor Martinez's lecture yesterday.

Raymond: Yeah, that was interesting. I've been hearing a lot more about allergies lately. I had no idea they were so serious and so common!

Elena: Right, and I was surprised to learn that when allergic reactions occur, the physical process is pretty much the same—whether it's a reaction to pollen or to peanuts.

Raymond: That surprised me, too. It sounds like the body mistakes the substance it's allergic to for something dangerous, and it tries to defend itself.

Elena: Mmm hmm. The body produces antibodies, and the antibodies attach themselves to mast cells. And when that happens, the mast cells do what they're supposed to do—they react!

Raymond: Exactly, but it turns out the cells are reacting to things that are not truly harmful.

Elena: Yeah, they are, at least they're harmful to some people—things like strawberries, peanuts, and chocolate—I'm allergic to all of those things.

Raymond: Wow—allergic to *chocolate*—that's really a shame.

Elena: It *is*. And how about you? Are you allergic to anything?

Raymond: No, at least not that I know of, *fortunately*!

Elena: Yeah, you're lucky. My allergies are really bad sometimes. Besides the food allergies, I have seasonal allergies. They can be pretty bad, especially in spring and early summer when the trees produce a lot of pollen, *and* I have *asthma*.

Raymond: Wow. You have *asthma* too? So living downtown can't be easy for you with all the air pollution.

Elena: Ugh, it isn't. The air pollution in this city is pretty bad. I also can't be around cats for very long, and some kinds of plants and flowers make my asthma act up, too. Fortunately, I respond well to my asthma medication. It works really quickly, and I always take it with me.

Raymond: Well that's good. What about your *food* allergies? I know those can be really serious for some people.

Elena: It's true. My food allergies are actually a much bigger problem for me. Like I said, I'm allergic to chocolate, strawberries, and peanuts. All things I *love*!

Raymond: I'd *hate* to be allergic to chocolate. I eat it every day.

Elena: Lucky you! Well, it's not easy, but being allergic to *peanuts* is actually harder because you don't always know when food contains peanuts or peanut oil.

Raymond: Good point. I never thought about it. But that reminds me, do you remember Professor Martinez talking about a "no-peanuts policy" here on campus?

Elena: Oh, yeah. And the cafeteria and snack bar both stopped serving anything with peanuts. Remember last year when that student had an allergic reaction and had to go to the hospital?

Raymond: Oh, right. I *remember* that. Professor Martinez called food allergies the "*new*" allergy problem.

Elena: Yeah, that's right. She said the research shows the number of children with food allergies rose 50 percent between 1997 and 2011, so it's a growing problem. I also read somewhere that between seven and eight percent of children nowadays have food allergies.

Raymond: Wow, that's a lot of kids! I wonder why so many of them have food allergies these days?

Elena: My doctor tells me that no one really knows, but there is a theory that the cause is partly genetic and partly environmental. In other words, our genes and our environment both play a role.

Unit 2: Technology Today and Tomorrow

LESSON A   Vocabulary

Track 1.11   A. Meaning from Context   Page 24

Timeline of AI History

1950: In *I, Robot*, a book of fictional short stories by Isaac Asimov, the makers of robots command them not to harm humans. The robots, however, sometimes create their own rules depending on the circumstances.

1950s: Computers become a practical tool for doing calculations quickly, and since they don't make any mistakes, they are more reliable than humans.

1956: Researchers at Dartmouth College say they intend to study "artificial intelligence" during a two-month summer conference.

1997: A computer called Deep Blue wins a chess match against world champion Garry Kasparov, and it's clear that computers can go beyond just following instructions and can actually "think" for themselves. In the past, programmers had to instruct computers in great detail and tell them exactly what to do.

2011: A computer called Watson replaces one of the humans competing on the TV quiz show *Jeopardy!*—and wins! Watson is capable of understanding spoken questions.

2016: Google puts together a group of engineers in Switzerland to research "machine learning," an important part of artificial intelligence.

Listening: A Radio Show about AI

Track 1.12   B. Listening for Main Ideas and   Page 26
              C. Note Taking   Page 27

Radio Host: Welcome back. As I mentioned before the break, Roger Ali is with us today to talk about artificial intelligence. Thank you for being here, Dr. Ali.

Roger Ali: Thank you for having me.

Radio Host: I'll be honest with you. When I hear the words "artificial intelligence," the first thing I think of is the character HAL from the movie *2001: A Space Odyssey*.

Roger Ali: Sure. Many people remember HAL. In the movie, he's the computer that controls the systems of a spacecraft. He also speaks with the people on the spacecraft.

Radio Host: And he's not very happy when the people decide to turn off the computer. In the movie, HAL becomes very dangerous.

Roger Ali: That's right, but fortunately, artificial intelligence in the *real* world isn't like HAL.

Radio Host: Well, that's good! Can you tell us what *is* happening in the field of AI?

Roger Ali: Many interesting things. For example, when we search for something on the Internet, the search results that we see are chosen carefully. The search engine has learned which websites are the most popular, the most reliable, and so on. This prevents us from seeing a lot of websites we're not really interested in.

Radio Host: In other words, the search engine *draws conclusions* about what we're looking for on the Internet.

Roger Ali: Right, so it only shows us the information it thinks we want to see, which includes advertisements as well. We usually see only ads for products that the computer thinks we might want to buy.

Radio Host: You said, "It *thinks*," but is the search engine *really* thinking?

Roger Ali: That depends on your definition of *thinking*. The search engine is capable of learning—*machine* learning—and it does have *knowledge*. Knowledge about the Internet. Are learning and knowledge part of your definition of thinking?

Radio Host: They're part of it, but human beings are capable of so much more. We have our senses—hearing, smell, sight, touch, taste—and our emotions. We notice a lot about the world, and we use our judgment to make decisions.

Roger Ali: That's true, and most computer scientists know that we can't replace human beings with computers. We don't intend to make robots for *every* kind of job, either. That's just not practical.

Radio Host: OK, but there are some jobs that robots *can* do.

Roger Ali: Yes, there are. I should probably explain this a little better. When we want a robot to do something, we need to instruct the robot in great detail. We enter information about what the robot is supposed to do in any situation. If we give the robot a command, or if it finds itself in certain circumstances, it knows *exactly* what to do, because we *told* it what to do!

Radio Host: That doesn't sound like a very intelligent machine.

Roger Ali: It's not, but the latest idea behind machine learning, or artificial intelligence, is that machines might someday act more like the human brain. We're trying to go beyond the idea of telling the machine everything. We want the machine to be able to learn and to tell *us* something new.

Radio Host: That sounds interesting, but what are machines going to tell us that we don't already know?

Roger Ali: We're not sure, but we hope that AI can be used in the medical field. Since computers can read a lot of information very quickly, they might be able to discover things that people don't have time to discover. If we think about cancer, for example, it's a problem for doctors because it's really *many* diseases—not just *one* disease. In addition, millions of people have had cancer, but doctors can't possibly know the facts about every one of those people.

Radio Host: But a computer could read all of that information and possibly see something that a human doctor couldn't see?

Roger Ali: That's our hope, but we're not there yet.

Radio Host: It's something for us to look forward to. Our guest today has been Roger Ali. Dr. Ali, thanks very much for joining us.

Roger Ali: It was my pleasure.

LESSON B Vocabulary

Track 1.13   A. Meaning from Context   Page 34

Saving the Environment in Germany

Germany has a history of caring about the environment, but it's a country with a lot of industry that consumes enormous amounts of coal. When coal and other fossil fuels such as petroleum are burned, they send carbon into the air, and carbon is the main cause of climate change. In order to fight air pollution and climate change, Germans have cut back on the amount of coal they use. As part of this effort, they are also using cleaner energy sources such as solar and wind power.

Innovative forms of technology, including enormous wind turbines and huge numbers of solar panels, are helping Germany reach its goal of having only 20 percent of its energy come from fossil fuels by the year 2050. The change has been gradual—beginning in the 1970s—and it hasn't been easy. Many environmental groups as well as individual people in Germany, have spent a lot of time and money on clean energy.

Changing Lives in India

Around 1.1 billion people worldwide live without electricity, and about 25 percent of those people live in India. Solar energy—in the form of small lights that get their power from the sun—is now solving problems for many of them. This innovative technology lets small businesses stay open at night, so people in India are earning more money. In addition to the positive economic impact, the air inside homes is cleaner since people are not burning wood or kerosene for light. Solar power is also a good alternative to expensive batteries that need to be replaced. With the help of innovative technology, people in rural villages can live more like people in large cities.

Listening: A Conversation about Technology

Track 1.14   A.   Page 36

Baltimore's Mr. Trash Wheel

With innovative technology, we can solve old problems in new ways. One old problem was the trash from the city of Baltimore, Maryland, that ended up in the Jones Falls River. The river flows into Baltimore's Inner Harbor—a popular tourist destination—and from there into the Chesapeake Bay and the Atlantic Ocean.

Meet Mr. Trash Wheel, a device that uses the motion of river water and energy from solar panels to collect plastic bottles, cigarette butts, carry-out food containers, and other garbage from the river. Baltimore's Inner Harbor is now a more attractive place for visitors. Hundreds of tons of trash have been removed from the water system, and other communities are thinking about building their own trash wheels.

Track 1.15   C. Listening for Main Ideas and   Page 37
D. Listening for Details

Scott: Too funny! Did you see this?

Jason: What are you looking at?

Scott: It's a funny post from Mr. Trash Wheel. He says he likes his job even though it's dirty and the work never ends!

Jason: Umm, Mr. *Trash Wheel*? Who's *that*?

Scott: Actually, it's a *what*, not a *who*. It's this big machine that collects trash from the river before it can go into Baltimore Harbor.

Jason: A big *machine*? So how does it work?

Scott: It has a water wheel on one side, so it gets its energy—or most of it—from water power, the movement of the water. That turns the wheel and makes the whole thing run, so it's not consuming any fossil fuels or producing any carbon.

Jason: Well, no carbon's a good thing.

Scott: Definitely! The trash just floats down the river to Mr. Trash Wheel and then it gets carried up a conveyer belt to a Dumpster, a big garbage container, and then when the Dumpster's full, the city takes it away. Here, take a look at the photo.

Jason: Wow, it's *big*, and it's kind of ugly! I mean, who wants to look at something like *that*?

Scott: Well, who cares what it *looks* like. It catches 90 percent of the trash from the river, and it's keeping the trash out of the Atlantic Ocean: millions of cigarette butts, plastic garbage bags, soda cans, you name it.

Jason: Right—all of that stuff that ends up in the ocean. It sounds like it's having a positive impact on the environment.

Scott: You got it. And a lot of people like Mr. Trash Wheel because of his social media presence. You can send him messages and interact with him online. In fact, a lot of people on the Internet said that he needed eyes, so they actually added two big eyes on the front! They're not in this photo, but you can see them if you go to the live feed.

Jason: There's a live feed? You mean I can go online and watch Mr. Trash Wheel clean garbage out of the river. *Fun!*

Scott: It *is* kind of fun! Maybe it's not the *best* way to spend your time, but you should check it out at least once.

Jason: Seriously, though, this is interesting because he's not really that high-tech. I mean, the water wheel's been around for hundreds of years. Solar panels are newer, but using the Internet and social media to make people *like* the technology—that's pretty innovative!

Scott: Right! He has a lot of followers online. And I think it's interesting that he works pretty independently. There's no worker or operator. Most of the time, there's no one there at all. It's a slow, gradual process, but it catches trash and cleans up the harbor.

Jason: OK, but here's my question. What if people just cut back on the amount of trash they throw into the river? Then they wouldn't need a trash wheel at all.

Scott: Well, it isn't that people are throwing trash into the river—well, not *most* people. They might throw trash into the street, though, and in Baltimore, that trash gets washed directly into the river every time it rains hard enough.

Jason: Oh, right. They have an old storm sewer system that goes directly into the river. This seems like a pretty smart system then. And certainly a cheaper alternative than building a new storm sewer system.

Scott: Yeah it is. In fact, several other communities worldwide are thinking about building their own Mr. Trash Wheel.

Jason: Interesting. I suppose that one individual trash wheel's helpful in one part of the world, but having a lot of these trash wheels in different places would increase the impact of the technology. Maybe they could build a *Ms.* Trash Wheel in one of those places?

Scott: Right, or maybe people could suggest names, post them online, and people could vote on them!

Jason: Hey, I like that idea!

Speaking

Track 1.16 Pronunciation: Stressed
Content Words   **Page 39**

The <u>book</u> is on the <u>table</u> in the <u>back</u> of the <u>room</u>.

My <u>friend</u> <u>took</u> a <u>chemistry</u> <u>course</u> in <u>college</u>.

Track 1.17 E.   **Page 39**

1. <u>Nabila</u> is <u>taking</u> a <u>course</u> in <u>computer programming</u>.
2. <u>Samir</u> wants to <u>become</u> a <u>software designer</u>.
3. All of my <u>friends</u> have <u>cell phones</u>.
4. <u>Large televisions</u> <u>consume</u> a <u>lot</u> of <u>electricity</u>.
5. I'm <u>trying</u> to <u>cut back</u> on the <u>time</u> I <u>spend</u> <u>online</u>.
6. <u>Kenji</u> wants to <u>buy</u> a <u>phone</u> with a <u>better</u> <u>camera</u>.

Unit 3: Culture and Tradition

LESSON A   Vocabulary

Track 1.18   A. Meaning from Context   **Page 44**

1. In my country, we have a custom of giving money to children on their birthdays. Parents usually give their children money as a gift.
2. The actual cost of a big holiday celebration can be higher than people expect. People often end up spending more money on food and gifts than they plan to.
3. Culture is a factor in gift giving. People from some cultures feel that if they receive a gift, they must give a gift in return. Their culture is a reason for that feeling.
4. Women in Japan still wear a kimono for their wedding. They haven't stopped wearing these beautiful clothes.
5. In Korea, people eat traditional foods, such as rice cakes, on New Year's Day. They have done this for a long time.
6. We are developing a program to teach foreigners about our culture. We are now making plans for this program.
7. In the future, many languages will probably disappear. Someday no one will speak these languages.
8. A group of people called the Inuit live in the Arctic regions of the world. They live in cold areas.
9. Many cultures use storytelling to help preserve their language and traditions. They tell stories to help keep them.
10. Scientists estimate that there are over 7,000 languages in the world. They don't know the exact number.

Track 1.19   C.   **Page 45**

Cowboy Life and Culture

In the 1800s, cowboys worked with cattle all across the Western region of the United States. An important factor in the cowboys' work was the long distance from cattle ranches to the nearest railroad. Cowboys moved cattle in huge cattle drives. It was hard work. Experts estimate that in a cattle drive, only about 10 cowboys would be involved in moving over 3,000 cattle.

Over time, cowboys developed some very interesting customs. For example, some cowboys would sing to their cattle at night to keep them quiet. Some traditional American songs were originally cowboy songs, and people still sing them today.

Cowboys have not disappeared completely: however, there are not nearly as many as there were in the past. And even though there are fewer actual cowboys now, many people in parts of the United States wear cowboy hats and boots. Rodeos are also very popular in some parts of the United States and help preserve some aspects of the cowboy culture.

Listening: A Lecture about Cowboys

Track 1.20   B. Listening for Main Ideas,   **Page 46**
C. Listening for Details, and   **Page 47**
D. Critical Thinking: Making
Inferences

Professor Diaz: OK, so let's get started. The cowboy way of life is one of the oldest traditions in North and South America. As you know, cattle eat grass—a *lot* of grass—so a herd, or *group* of cattle, must be moved often to new places with more grass. The people who move the cattle are called *cowboys*.

A lot of people today think that the last cowboys disappeared a long time ago, and it's true that there are fewer cowboys today than in the past. Money is one factor in this because cowboys usually *don't* earn a lot of money for all the hard work they do. But in some places, cowboys still ride their horses as they move cattle to places with more grass. They also still practice traditional cowboy customs such as sleeping outdoors under the stars and singing songs near campfires at night. Their way of life hasn't changed much over time because their work hasn't really changed.

Today we'll talk about two regions in North America that still have cowboys—the western United States and Mexico. And thanks to a fascinating book on this topic by a National Geographic photographer named Robb Kendrick, we'll be able to look at two actual cowboys from those places. Kendrick's book is called *Still: Cowboys at the Start of the Twenty-First Century*. As he was writing the book, Kendrick interviewed modern cowboys in different places, and he used a very old kind of camera to photograph the cowboys.

The first cowboy we'll look at lives in the U.S. His name is Tyrel Tucker. He was 18 years old when Kendrick took this photo. Tyrel was born in Wyoming and was riding horses before he could walk. He got his first horse when he was just two years old! According to Kendrick, Tyrel started working as a cowboy during his school vacations and developed a love for being outdoors.

He eventually left school to help with the family ranch and was happy to do that. While all of his classmates were indoors studying and playing computer games, Tyrel was working outside. As you might guess, however, living away from home and the actual work of a cowboy can be quite difficult. In Kendrick's book, Tyrel describes one winter when he and his older brother, Blaine, were working on a ranch in Arizona. He estimates they took care of *2,300* cattle there, so it was a big job! Tyrel and Blaine were the only people on the ranch. They lived in a very small house—a shack, really—with no electricity and ate pancakes, potatoes, and hamburgers every day. But even so, Tyrel enjoyed the work.

Kendrick also interviewed cowboys in Mexico. The cowboy tradition there began in the 1600s, when Spanish people brought the first cattle to the New World. In Mexico, large ranches needed workers to take care of their herds of cattle. These men were called *vaqueros*, from the Spanish word *vaca*, which means cow. The *vaqueros* worked outdoors in the hot sun, so they started wearing big hats to keep the sun off their faces and high boots to protect their legs. Later, some Mexican *vaqueros* moved north into Texas, and their clothing—hats and boots—became a part of the cowboy culture there, too. Wearing cowboy hats and boots is a custom that people have preserved in many parts of North America.

These days, there are two kinds of cowboys in Mexico. *Vaqueros* work with cattle on the ranches, especially in the northern region of the country. They still ride horses and live outdoors for many months at a time. In addition, Mexico also has *charros*, and they're an important part of popular culture in Mexico. *Charros* wear beautiful cowboy clothing, ride horses, and compete in sporting events called *charreadas*. Most *charros* don't work on ranches, but they are part of the cowboy tradition in Mexico—a tradition that has been preserved and continues to this day.

Manuel Rodriguez is one of the Mexican cowboys that Kendrick interviewed for his book. He was working as a *vaquero* in Coahuila, Mexico, when Kendrick met him. Manuel started his work as a vaquero early in life. He started helping his father at La Mora Ranch when he was only *four years old*. His parents, his grandparents, and even his great-grandparents have all worked at La Mora Ranch. When Kendrick took this photo, Manuel had recently gotten married and moved to the city, but he was planning to move back to the countryside and work as a *vaquero* again after his first child was born.

OK, so these examples from Kendrick's book show us that there *are* still cowboys in North America today who are part of a very old tradition.

Speaking

Track 1.21   A.   Pages 48–49

Emily: During the lecture, you said that the cowboy tradition in Mexico began in the 1600s. Could you please explain the situation there today?

Professor Diaz: Certainly. Some cowboys in Mexico are workers who live with the cattle and take care of them. The ranches there can be very large, and cattle need to be moved from place to place, so there are still cowboys working in Mexico today.

Liam: You talked about *two* kinds of cowboys in Mexico. Could you explain them again?

Professor Diaz: Sure. The most famous cowboys in Mexico are the *charros*. They ride their horses in contests called *charreadas*. The other kind of cowboys are the *vaqueros*—the ones who work with cattle every day.

Liam: I'm afraid I still don't understand. What kind of work do *charros* do, exactly?

Professor Diaz: I'll put it another way. For *charros*, riding horses and roping cattle is mostly a sport, or a hobby. *Charros* have many of the same skills as any cowboy, and they perform those skills for an audience in the *charreada* events. But for the *vaqueros*, this is their job. It's how they make a living.

Liam: OK. So, Manuel Rodriguez, the cowboy in the book, is a *vaquero*, not a *charro*, right?

Professor Diaz: Exactly!

Emily: Just to clarify, do you mean that *charros* aren't real cowboys?

Professor Diaz: No, I said that *charros are* a part of the cowboy tradition, but many of them don't do it as actual work.

LESSON B   Vocabulary

Track 1.22   A. Meaning from Context   Page 54

Anthropology 106: Culture and Music

Assignment: Oral Presentation

For this assignment, you will select a kind of music from another country and teach your classmates about it. Your presentation should be at least two minutes.

- Describe how the music sounds. Does it have a nice melody? Is the rhythm fast or slow? What kinds of instruments do the musicians play? Are there typically singers and lyrics? Play an example of the music so your audience can hear it.
- Explain where and when people typically listen to this kind of music. Do they listen to it on special occasions, such as weddings or holidays?
- Compare this kind of music to another kind of music you know about. How are they similar? Then contrast the two kinds of music. How are they different?
- Define any words you think your classmates may not know.
- In your conclusion, summarize the different aspects of the music that you discussed and remind your audience of the most important ideas of your presentation.

Listening: An Assignment about Music

Track 1.23   B. Note Taking   Page 57

Professor: OK. In class yesterday, we were listening to music from Latin America. We heard some traditional music, and we also heard some examples of new, modern music that developed from that music. Now I'm going to ask *you* to do some research and give a short presentation in class. C'mon, you'll all do a great job, I'm sure. OK, I'd like you to do six things for this presentation assignment, so please listen up and take notes. First, you'll need to select a kind of music from another culture to present. Then, in your presentation, I want you to talk a little bit about the culture this music comes from. Got that? Next you should describe the music and explain which aspects of it are traditional and which aspects are new, or modern. Remember to define any words we might not know. Then I want you to compare and contrast it with another kind of music we've talked about in class this semester. I'd also like you to play a sample of the music if you can. And finally, in your conclusion, you should briefly summarize the main ideas of your presentation. Oh, and you should also allow a few minutes at the end for questions. OK? Everyone got that? You'll give your presentations in class next Thursday and Friday. Now, unless there are any questions about that, I'd like to . . .

Female student: Excuse me, I have a question. How long should our presentations be?

Professor: Right, that's important! Thank you. Your presentations should be about two to three minutes.

Male student: Umm, sorry, I have a question—what do you mean by *aspects*? You said we should explain which *aspects* of the music are traditional.

Professor: By that I mean things like the instruments, the rhythm, the melody, the lyrics, and so on.

Male student: OK. Thanks.

Professor: Any other questions? No? OK, see you Thursday.

Track 1.24   C. Listening for Main Ideas   Page 57

Student: Good morning. I'm Alex, as you know. and I'm going to talk to you today about music from the Roma culture, specifically, the music by a group called Shukar Collective. They're from Romania, and I first heard their music when I was living in Greece.

I really liked it then, and I still like it now. OK, first, I just wanted to define the word *Shukar*. It means "fine" or "really good" in the Romani language. And I think they're really good, so I think it's a good name for them.

Shukar Collective is a group of musicians and DJs from Eastern Europe. They were very active from around 2005 until 2010. At that time they were playing a lot, and they were making recordings and music videos. They play music from the Roma people. So, about the Roma culture . . . Traditionally, the Roma people didn't have a country of their own, so they moved frequently from place to place. Now, they mostly stay in one place, and many of them speak two languages—their own Roma language and the language of the country where they live.

One thing the Roma people are very famous for is music. Traditional Roma music usually has a very fast rhythm, and the song lyrics express very strong feelings. OK, the instruments,... The traditional Roma instruments are drums and an instrument called the *cimbalom;* it sounds sort of like a piano. Shukar Collective also uses some new, electronic instruments, so their music is a mixture of traditional and modern sounds. I *really* like their music as you can probably tell. The group is made up of *three* traditional singers and *four* electronic musicians. They call their music *electro-gypsy-dance*. I actually did not bring a sample of their music to play today. I forgot, but I can bring one in tomorrow, or you can probably just go online and find some of their music. OK, so to summarize: Shukar Collective is a group from Eastern Europe. They play music from the Roma culture, which combines traditional and new, electronic sounds. It has been popular in Europe. Well, that's it. Thanks for listening to my presentation. . So, does anyone have any questions?

Speaking

Track 1.25   **Pronunciation: Reduced Function Words**   **Page 59**

The sound *of a* steel drum *is* light *and* happy.
We bought *a* birthday gift *for* Molly.
What are *you* reading? *Can* I *see* it?

Track 1.26   **D.**   **Page 59**

1. The violin is my favorite instrument.
2. Our friends are waiting outside.
3. Only a few people play this kind of guitar.
4. You can probably hear it on the radio.
5. The group is playing in a small theater.
6. Tell Maria about the class assignment.

Unit 4: A Thirsty World

LESSON A   Vocabulary

Track 1.27   **A. Meaning from Context**   **Page 64**

QUIZ: How much do you know about water?

1. The Amazon River supplies about 20% of the fresh water that enters the world's oceans.
2. Farmers require 911 gallons (3,450 liters) of water to produce 2.2 pounds (1 kilogram) of rice.
3. The risk of disease is high if the water you drink is not clean. About 1 million people die each year from drinking dirty water.
4. Farming uses a significant amount of water—up to 40 percent of the fresh water used worldwide.
5. The United States has built more than 80,000 dams to manage water for different uses such as producing electricity.
6. Scientists say that 13 gallons (50 liters) of water per day is adequate for one person.
7. You can collect water in a desert with just a sheet of plastic and an empty can.
8. Water is a renewable resource, so we can use the same water again and again.
9. The Nile River in Africa (the longest river in the world) flows through four different countries.
10. People in Australia use the smallest amount of water of any country in the world.

Listening: A Talk about the Itaipu Dam

Track 1.28   **B. Listening for Main Ideas and**   **Page 66**
              C. Note Taking   **Page 67**

Guest Speaker: Well, good afternoon everyone. Thank you for inviting me to speak to you today, and thank you all for coming. I'm here to talk to you about the Itaipu Dam, located near the border between Brazil and Paraguay, not far from a series of fantastic waterfalls in the Iguaçu National Park.

Today, I'm going to discuss both the *benefits* that the dam has brought to Brazil and Paraguay, as well as some of the *problems* it has caused. The Itaipu Dam is, of course, a great engineering achievement. It consists of four sections, which total nearly five miles across. It's one of the largest dams in the world. The reservoir behind the dam, which collects and holds the water from the Paraná River, is about 100 miles long. It's truly enormous!

As you can probably imagine, building a dam this size was quite a task. They actually had to *change* the course of the Paraná River while they were building the dam. This required about 40,000 workers, so a lot of jobs were created. But it's not only the size of the dam that's impressive. Its benefits to the region are impressive, too.

The Itaipu Dam provides about 20% of the electricity used in Brazil and about 75% of the electricity used in Paraguay. That electricity goes to millions of homes and businesses, so it's good for the economy of both countries. The dam has also become a major tourist attraction, which is good for the economy as well. Visitors to the dam can go on free tours. They can also go sightseeing in the beautiful natural areas near the dam.

Another important benefit is that Brazil and Paraguay are now able to manage one of their most valuable resources—the water that flows in the Paraná River. Drought can be a real problem for farmers and other people living in the region. Fortunately, the reservoir behind the dam supplies a large amount of water for irrigation—water that farmers can use to grow food.

Now, as is the case with any large dam, there are risks associated with the Itaipu Dam. For example, when the reservoir behind the dam was filled up, it covered more than 520 square miles of land with water. It's really a large lake now. As a result, around 10,000 families—perhaps as many as 50,000 people—lost their land and had to leave the area and find new homes. Historical and cultural sites are now underwater too because of the dam. Archaeologists are quite upset about this, and with good reason.

Other people are concerned about how the dam is affecting the environment. Besides the forest areas that were lost when the dam was built, farmers nearby are saying that the water in the reservoir is affecting the local climate—by actually raising air temperatures by about four degrees Celsius. They're saying the water in the reservoir heats up with energy from the sun, and in a warm part of the world, that's not a good thing for farmers. And speaking of heat and drought, in some years the amount of water in the river has been much lower than normal. This reduces the amount of energy the dam can produce.

Perhaps the most significant disadvantage of the Itaipu Dam has to do with the agreement between Brazil and Paraguay. It's a bi-national project, and both countries should be sharing the energy and the money generated by the dam. But not everyone thinks that the agreement is fair. There were some changes to that agreement in 2009, and more changes will be needed in 2023 when the agreement ends. Hopefully both countries will be happy with those changes, and both countries will share equally in the benefits from the dam.

So, as we can see, although the Itaipu Dam has caused some serious problems in the region, its benefits are more significant, since it helps solve two of the biggest problems in the area: the energy demands of two growing countries and not having adequate water for farming. Major problems like these often require large-scale solutions, and the Itaipu Dam is an example of this. Again, thank you all very much for coming today. Now, are there any questions?

Speaking

Track 1.29   Pronunciation: Suffixes and Syllable Stress   Page 69

educate → educ**a**tion

industry → ind**us**trial

av**ai**lable → availab**i**lity

history → hi**stor**ical

Track 1.30   D.   Page 69

1. politics   It was a significant political event.
2. resident   This is a residential apartment building.
3. apply   We turned in our application before the due date.
4. possible   There is a possibility of finding water on other planets.
5. inform   We need more information before we make a decision.
6. theory   This is only a theoretical situation. It's not real.

LESSON B   Vocabulary

Track 1.31   B. Meaning from Context   Page 74

1. An urgent problem in the western United States is low levels of groundwater.

2. Water from rivers can be distributed to cities and farms where the water is needed.
3. Without adequate water for agriculture, a world food crisis is possible. If farmers do not have enough water for their crops, it could affect millions of people.
4. Farmers can reduce the amount of water they use. Learning about and practicing water conservation will allow them to do the same work with less water.
5. Parts of northern Africa are extremely dry. For example, the average yearly rainfall in the Sahara Desert is less than 1 inch (25 mm).
6. Water is scarce in many regions of the world, and people in these areas often do not have access to clean water.
7. Australia has experienced both drought and floods in recent years. This has been very difficult for the farmers there.

Listening: A Discussion about the Ogallala Aquifer

**Track 1.32   B. Listening for Main Ideas and   Page 76
                C. Listening for Problems   Page 77
                and Solutions**

Paula: Hi, Ron.

Ron: How's it going, Paula?

Paula: Oh, hey Taylor.

Taylor: Hi.

Paula: Well, I'm glad we could get together today. Our group presentation is next Thursday—yikes! Anyway, I found an interesting article about the Ogallala Aquifer in the western region of the United States.

Ron: Really? Where in the west? I was born in Oklahoma.

Paula: That's great. That's one of the states they mention in the article. There are some really good photos of agriculture in the region. Maybe we can include some of them in our slides. Look, here's a great photo of a farm in Kansas.

Taylor: Wow! That's a lot of corn! Is it for feeding cattle?

Paula: Yeah. The article says that there are over 500 cattle on this farm. Here, Taylor, take a look.

Taylor: Thanks. Oh, I see. Wow! That's a lot of cattle!

Ron: Yeah, it sounds like they're doing pretty well. So, what's the problem? The topic for our presentation is "How to Solve the Aquifer Crisis." It doesn't seem like *that* farm is experiencing a crisis. I guess I'm not very clear on what we're supposed to talk about in our presentation. I mean, what *is* the aquifer crisis, anyway?

Taylor: It's the situation that Professor Arnold covered in class last week. She talked about the aquifers, you know, the water that's in the ground. Since water from rain or rivers is scarce in some places, a lot of water is pumped up out of the ground for irrigation to grow crops for food. And when that water is gone, it's *gone*.

Ron: Hmmm. That must have been the day I was out sick. It sounds like I missed some important information. OK, so, go on.

Paula: Right, so some crops like corn need a lot of water to grow, and some of the western states in the U.S. are extremely dry. The average rainfall in Colorado, for example, is only 15 inches for the whole year. Compare that to Illinois, where they get around 40 inches of rain a year. I think I'd rather be a corn farmer in Illinois!

Taylor: Clearly 15 inches a year is not a lot of rain, but is it really an urgent situation when we have such a huge aquifer? After all, it sits underneath eight *big* western states! And the water is helping people because it's used to grow crops, right?

Paula: Right, the water is being used to grow crops, but the Ogallala Aquifer took around 15,000 years to fill up.

Taylor: Wow! Really?

Paula: Yeah, and the problem is that farmers and other people in the region have pumped the water out very quickly. It's only been in the past 70 years or so. Now there's much less water in the aquifer. Some people in western states don't even have water at their homes for drinking or washing.

Taylor: Wow! That sounds pretty bad—not having adequate clean water at home? I can't imagine not being able to take a shower every day.

Ron: We've been lucky, I guess. I don't think we've ever experienced a serious water shortage around here. It must be difficult for those people without water at home, but I think growing food is an even more important issue. People need to eat!

Paula: True. So having enough water to grow food is also a problem, and that's why we need to think about the solutions we're going to talk about in our presentation.

Ron: What does the article say? Can farmers use water from rivers and streams to irrigate their crops instead of taking water from the aquifer?

Paula: That's one possible solution, but unfortunately, rivers and streams are often far away, and it's quite difficult and expensive to distribute water to large areas across long distances. Still, it's a possible solution for some people—just not for everyone.

Taylor: Hmmm. What if farmers in the west just reduced the amount of water they take from the aquifer? Then the water that's there would last longer.

Ron: That's a smart solution. We had some neighbors in Oklahoma who did something called "dryland farming." They grew wheat, but they didn't use any irrigation.

Taylor: Huh. That's interesting. Why didn't they need to irrigate?

Ron: With dryland farming, they plant crops that don't need much water. They also follow good water and soil conservation practices. For example, they plant the seeds at very specific times of year to take advantage of what little rain they get. And to prevent the dry dirt, or soil, from blowing away, they plant trees to block, or break, the wind. One year my father and I helped our neighbors plant trees. They call it a "windbreak."

Paula: Interesting. I've never heard of "dryland farming." It makes a lot of sense, and your personal experience with it would be good information for the presentation. In the real world, though, would everyone agree on the idea? The farmers who are raising corn and cattle are making a good living. They might not want to change.

Taylor: OK, but for our presentation at least, let's focus on these two possible solutions: number one, better ways to distribute water from rivers and streams and number two, water conservation—for example, through dryland farming.

Paula: Sounds good! Both of those would help to solve the problems of not having enough water for homes and not enough water for crops. Now, let's decide which photos to include in our slides.

CD 2

Unit 5: Inside the Brain

LESSON A   Vocabulary

Track 2.2   A. Meaning from Context   Page 84

Facts to Make You Think about Your Brain

1. Your brain is an extremely complex organ. It contains over 100 billion neurons that are constantly sending messages. Different neurons send messages at different speeds—some faster and some slower.
2. Every time you experience something new, your brain creates new connections and pathways between brain cells.
3. The common belief that we use only a tiny amount (10 percent) of our brains is wrong. Each part of the brain has a function, so we use 100 percent of our brains.
4. Even without words, you can figure out how someone is feeling. A part of your brain called the *amygdala* lets you "read" other people's faces and understand what kind of mood they are in.
5. Every time you think, laugh, or sneeze, chemical and electrical signals are moving between neurons. These messages make it possible for your brain to communicate with your body.
6. Learning changes the structure of the brain. When you learn a new skill, such as playing a musical instrument, your brain cells organize themselves in a new way.
7. Your brain is extremely powerful. When you're awake, it generates between 10 and 23 watts of electricity—enough to power a light bulb!
8. The *hypothalamus* is the part of your brain that controls body temperature. It keeps you from getting too hot or too cold.

Listening: A Podcast about Exercise and the Brain

Track 2.3   B. Listening for Main Ideas and   Page 86
C. Listening for Details   Page 87

Aaron Fleming: Welcome back to the podcast. I'm Aaron Fleming, and I'm talking today with Jocelyn Taylor. Our goal today is to make you think about the human brain.

Jocelyn Taylor: That's right, Aaron. More specifically, we're talking about the effects of *exercise* on the brain.

Aaron Fleming: Great. Let's get started. I'm guessing you're going to tell us that exercise is *good* for the brain.

Jocelyn Taylor: Yes, there's really no surprise there, I suppose. Exercise—anything that makes your heart beat faster—is not only good for your body, but good for your brain as well.

Aaron Fleming: I've heard exercise can put us in a better mood—make us feel better mentally and emotionally.

Jocelyn Taylor: That's true, and scientists learned recently that exercise makes you *smarter* as well.

Aaron Fleming: I know a lot of people who are going to be happy to hear that! All of my friends who are out there jogging or playing tennis every day.

Jocelyn Taylor: They're doing the right thing! That's because for some time *after* you've exercised, your body produces a chemical that actually makes it easier for your brain to *learn*.

Aaron Fleming: Wait, now in order to *learn* something, don't you just need to repeat it several times? For example, my son is learning to ride a bicycle. He practices near our house—with some help from me, of course—and when he does, his brain sends him "bike riding" messages along certain pathways in his brain. Eventually, he'll know how to ride a bike— no problem!

Jocelyn Taylor: That's right, and those bike-riding messages form new connections between the neurons in your son's brain. In fact, the structure of our brain actually *changes* every time we learn something new.

Aaron Fleming: So let's get back to exercise. I know my mood is better after I exercise, but I'm not sure it's making me any smarter.

Jocelyn Taylor: Let me explain. You probably know that your brain generates some electricity.

Aaron Fleming: Right, and electrical signals are moving inside the brain. That's what makes it possible for us to move, or think, or have conversations like this one.

Jocelyn Taylor: Exactly, but it's a little more complex than that. Those signals in the brain are part electricity and part chemistry. Whenever you have a thought or perform any kind of action, it's because tiny chemical and electrical signals are moving at high speeds inside your brain. It's as if you have billions of tiny neuron highways inside your head.

Aaron Fleming: OK, I think I understand the function of the neurons. They're like wires inside an electrical device. They carry the messages around the brain—and between the brain and the rest of the body. But the brain is *not* an electrical device.

Jocelyn Taylor: No, it's not. A lot of the brain's functions have to do with chemicals.

Aaron Fleming: And what's the chemical that's produced when we exercise?

Jocelyn Taylor: It's called *BDNF*, and it's really important for memory and learning. The reason for this is that BDNF controls some of the *processes* in the brain, such as the way the brain grows new neurons.

Aaron Fleming: So, if this chemical affects memory and learning, I can see why you said it makes us smarter. And is exercise the only way to get it? I mean, can't you just buy it at the store or something?

Jocelyn Taylor: No, sorry, Aaron. BDNF is only made in the brain, and it's the result of regular exercise. And you need to exercise several times a week.

Aaron Fleming: Well then, I guess I'd better keep exercising! I want to keep my *brain* fit as well as my body.

Jocelyn Taylor: I'm with you on that!

Aaron Fleming: My thanks to Jocelyn Taylor for being with me today. I've enjoyed speaking with you.

Jocelyn Taylor: My pleasure, Aaron. Thanks for having me.

Speaking

Track 2.4   Pronunciation: Linking   Page 89

It's a fascinating job.

I knew it was the right answer.

The book will certainly be interesting.

What was your reason for leaving?

Track 2.5   D.   Page 89

1. Your brain controls everything you do.
2. Your brain generates enough energy to power a light bulb.

3. The activity in your brain never stops.
4. I'm with you on that!
5. Any exercise that makes your heart beat faster can help your mood.
6. Neurons carry the messages around the brain.

LESSON B   Vocabulary

Track 2.6   A. Meaning from Context   Page 94

Romantic Love vs. Long-Term Attachments

There are many different kinds of love. There is the strong emotion we feel when we fall in love. There is the attachment between parents and children, and the quiet feeling of security that develops slowly in long-term relationships, when couples are together for many years.

Your brain knows the difference between romantic love and other attachments. When we're in love, the amount of a brain chemical called *dopamine* increases. This increase gives us the extra energy we feel when we're in love.

On the other hand, an increase in dopamine can make the brains of people in love similar to the brains of people with OCD—Obsessive Compulsive Disorder. People with OCD cannot stop thinking about something, and these thoughts can cause compulsive behaviors—actions the person cannot control, such as washing the hands again and again. Similarly, people who are in love often cannot stop thinking about the person they are in love with. Both kinds of people may find it difficult to function normally because of their thoughts.

Fortunately, this "lovesickness" is a short-term condition. With time, strong romantic feelings decrease, and we can concentrate on "real life" again. As time passes, couples have higher levels of *oxytocin*—a brain chemical connected with calm feelings of happiness and trust.

So is love only a matter of brain chemistry? In fact, while chemicals do affect the way we feel, psychological factors are also important. We might be attracted to someone who likes the same things we like, for example, or someone who makes us feel safe and secure.

Listening: A Discussion about Memory, Learning, and Emotions

Track 2.7   B. Listening for Main Ideas and   Page 96
C. Listening for Details

Toshi: I'm glad we decided to form a study group. I always find it helpful to study with other people.

Julia: I agree. Studying in a group definitely helps me. Thanks for suggesting it, Toshi.

Liz: Yes, thank you, Toshi. And Julia, your idea to divide the topics and summarize the information in our notes was brilliant as well!

Julia: Well, I'm glad it was helpful. Maybe you could go first, Liz.

Liz: Absolutely. My topic was memory, or how do we remember things? According to my notes, the memory process has three steps. OK, first, information enters the brain through our senses— what we taste, smell, touch, see, and hear—and it is stored, *kept* there for a very short time—less than a second. OK, so *then*, only *some* of this information moves to our short-term memory.

Toshi: Sorry, Liz, can I interrupt for a second? Could you explain why we don't remember everything? I mean, I know from experience that we don't, but why don't we?

Liz: Hmmm. I'm actually not sure why, but Professor Wong said that only the information we need to use immediately moves to our short-term memory.

Julia: Right. I remember that. Our short-term memory allows us to function normally in the world. For example, if you ask me a question, I can remember the question long enough to answer it.

Liz: Right, but you might not remember the question tomorrow. OK, the third and final part of the memory process happens when information that we *try* to remember, or that our *brain* decides is important, moves to our *long*-term memory. This information can last a *lifetime*.

Toshi: Right, and if you really want to remember something, you need to think about it, or say it, or do it many times. Memories become stronger when they are sent down the same pathway in the brain many times, And yes, I remember *that* from the lecture!

Julia: Thanks, you two. That was helpful. Now, before I give you my summary, let's go back to what Toshi just said. If you want to remember something, and you concentrate on it and think about it and repeat it again and again, that's very similar to actually *learning* something, right?

Liz: That's right. Here's what I wrote in my notes: "To *remember* is to recall the past. To *learn* is to do something differently in the future."

Julia: Huh. That's a good way to look at it. To learn new information, you have to concentrate on it and think about it. Or to learn how to *do* something, like ride a bicycle, you have to do it again and again.

Toshi: It's interesting to me that when you learn new things, your brain forms new connections—new pathways of neurons. So learning actually *changes* the structure of the brain! That's pretty amazing.

Julia: Yeah, pretty interesting stuff!

Toshi: Alright, so I guess it's my turn now. Ready? My topic was emotions and the brain, especially the emotions of romantic love and feelings of attachment and security. This was quite interesting to me because I think of emotions as being psychological. They're the result of our past experiences and our nature—probably even the way our parents raised us. But in fact, emotions are also *chemical*, not just psychological. There's a chemical in our brains called dopamine, for example, and the level of dopamine increases when we fall in love with someone.

Track 2.8   D. Note Taking   Page 97

Toshi: I'm glad we decided to form a study group. I always find it helpful to study with other people.

Julia: I agree. Studying in a group definitely helps me. Thanks for suggesting it, Toshi.

Liz: Yes, thank you, Toshi. And Julia, your idea to divide the topics and summarize the information in our notes was brilliant as well!

Julia: Well, I'm glad it was helpful. Maybe you could go first, Liz.

Liz: Absolutely. My topic was memory, or how do we remember things? According to my notes, the memory process has three steps. OK, first, information enters the brain through our senses—what we taste, smell, touch, see, and hear—and it is stored, *kept* there for a very short time—less than a second. OK, so *then,* only *some* of this information moves to our short-term memory.

Toshi: Sorry, Liz, can I interrupt for a second? Could you explain why we don't remember everything? I mean, I know from experience that we don't, but why don't we?

Liz: Hmmm. I'm actually not sure why, but Professor Wong said that only the information we need to use immediately moves to our short-term memory.

Julia: Right. I remember that. Our short-term memory allows us to function normally in the world. For example, if you ask me a question, I can remember the question long enough to answer it.

Liz: Right, but you might not remember the question tomorrow. OK, the third and final part of the memory process happens when information that we *try* to remember, or that the *brain* decides is important, moves to our *long*-term memory. This information can last a *lifetime*.

Unit 6: Let's Eat!

LESSON A   Vocabulary

Track 2.9   A.   Page 104

grains	protein	servings	specific
guidelines	recommend	source	varied
modernize	regional		

Track 2.10   B. Meaning from Context   Page 104

1. Today, many countries have produced guidelines to teach their citizens about healthy diets.
2. Most doctors recommend eating a lot of fruits and vegetables.
3. Grains such as rice, wheat, and corn are basic parts of most people's diets.
4. It's OK to include a few servings of sweets in your diet each week, but not too many.
5. Cheese is an excellent source of calcium; so are milk and yogurt.
6. Scientists believe the regional food in Sardinia, Italy, helps the people who live there to have long, healthy lives.
7. A varied diet includes many different kinds of food, not just the same foods again and again.
8. Foods that are high in protein include fish, chicken, nuts, and beans.
9. This recipe calls for a specific kind of red pepper. You can't use just any kind of pepper.
10. To modernize means to begin using the newest technology and methods.

Listening: A Presentation about the Korean Diet

Track 2.11   B. Listening for Main Ideas and Page 106
D. Listening for Numerical   Page 107
Data

Mi-Ran: Hello, everyone. As you know, I'm from South Korea, and people from my country love food! So today I'll be talking about—what else? Food! Specifically, I'll be talking about changes in the Korean diet in the twentieth century. First, as you might know, South Korea is a country that developed very quickly. Around 50 years ago, South Korea was a developing agricultural country. Today, it's one of the most modern countries in Asia. And people's diets have modernized, too. In my research, I've been looking at these dietary changes and trying to answer this question: which kind of diet is better—a traditional diet or a modern one?

OK, this chart shows what Koreans ate in two different years: 1969, before Korea started modernizing, and 1995, after Korea was modernized. You can see that in 1969, people were eating about 37 ounces of food every day, and in 1995, they were eating about 39 ounces of food. That's not a very big change. So, even when Korea was a developing country, overall, people had enough food.

Male student: Mi-Ran, may I say something here? Um, you're talking about the average amount of food, so maybe some people really *didn't* have enough to eat. Can we really assume that *everyone* was eating well?

Mi-Ran: That's a good point. Actually, because Korea was a farming country then, almost everyone had *some* kind of food, but their diets weren't always healthy. OK, Moving on, when we compare the *kinds* of food people ate, we see a significant difference. The most important food in Korea is rice: we eat it three times a day. In 1969, people were eating 20 ounces of rice every day—more than a pound! That's a *lot* of rice—around six servings per day. But if you don't eat a varied diet, you are not going to be very healthy. By 1995, people were eating only 11 ounces of rice and other grains per day—much less than in the past. Now, remember, the total amount of food increased during that period of time. So, what specific foods *were* people eating in 1995?

If you look at the chart, you'll see that people were eating more of *everything*. Their diets became much more varied. The amount of vegetables they ate increased a little from 9 and a half ounces a day in 1969, to 10 ounces a day in 1995. But people were eating a *lot* more fruit. The amount of fruit people ate increased from about 2 ounces a day to about 5 ounces a day. They were getting more vitamins from that extra fruit. And look at meat. In 1969, people were eating only a very tiny amount of meat—about a quarter of an ounce a day. In 1995, they were eating almost two and a half ounces a day. That's ten times as much. Finally, look at the numbers for milk. OK, in 1969, people were only drinking about one tenth of an ounce of milk per day. In 1995, that increased to about 2.3 ounces a day. All in all, Korean people's diets in 1995 were much closer to government guidelines than they used to be.

Female student: Could I ask a question, Mi-Ran? Is that just milk, or does that include other dairy products too?

Mi-Ran: That includes all dairy products. A lot of Koreans like yogurt and ice cream, though there are regional differences. People in different parts of the country like to eat different things; it varies.

Mi-Ran: Alright. To continue, as the country developed, instead of just eating a lot of rice and vegetables, Koreans started including many other kinds of food in their diets, especially animal products like meat, fish, eggs, and dairy products. One reason for this change was that people had more money, so they could buy more of these expensive foods. The percentage of animal products in the Korean diet went from 3 percent in 1969 to almost 21 percent in 1995! That's the biggest change in the Korean diet.

Now, some nutritionists recommend having a diet that consists of mostly plant foods such as grains and fruits and vegetables. They think animal products—meat, cheese, butter, and so on—aren't healthy. But I'm not sure those nutritionists are totally correct. That's because young Koreans today are taller than before. The average height of teenage boys is about 3 and a half inches taller. And the average teenage girl is almost 2 inches taller. It's very interesting! I think that young people now are taller because of the improved diet. Meat, milk, cheese, and other animal products are good sources of protein. And if a population eats more protein, people are taller on average. Really, in general, people in Korea are healthier now.

So, in conclusion, I want to return to my original question: Which is better—a modern diet or a traditional diet? Now, in some of the other presentations, we heard about places where the modern diet has caused some new health problems. But my research on South Korea shows us that in some ways, at least, a modern diet can be better than a traditional diet. Thank you very much. Does anyone have any questions?

Speaking

Track 2.12   D.   Page 109

1. **Male student:** Mi-Ran, may I say something here?
2. **Mi Ran:** Moving on, when we compare the kinds of food people ate, we see a significant difference.
3. **Female student:** Could I ask a question, Mi-Ran? Is that just milk, or does that include other dairy products too?
4. **Mi Ran:** To continue, as the country developed, instead of just eating a lot of rice and vegetables, Koreans started including many other kinds of food in their diets, . . .

Track 2.13   Pronunciation Intonation: Finished and Unfinished Sentences   Page 110

I have to go to the supermarket.

She lives in Tokyo.

I saw Pam yesterday…

Mike's brother called…

Track 2.14   E.   Page 110

1. I really don't like milk.
2. Rick has two favorite restaurants…
3. I'll buy chicken if it looks fresh…
4. On my next vacation, I want to go to Seoul.
5. My mother is an excellent cook…
6. If the weather is nice, we usually go to the park.

LESSON B   Vocabulary

Track 2.15   A. Meaning from Context   Page 114

Dr. Alia Crum's Milkshake Experiment

Introduction:

We know that seeing a picture of food can make us hungry, but Dr. Crum, a psychologist and researcher, wanted to find out whether reading food labels can affect the body. Her conclusion was that our attitude is relevant to the way our bodies respond to food.

To understand this experiment, it is important to understand the hormone *ghrelin*. When you have not eaten, the level of ghrelin in your body rises. It stimulates feelings of hunger and "tells" us we need to eat. After we have eaten enough, the level drops, we feel full, and our bodies use the food for energy and strength.

Results:

Dr. Crum's research strategy was to give two groups of people the same milkshake but with two different labels. First, the team asked participants to read the label on the milkshake. Then participants drank the milkshake and rated the taste. The final step was a blood test.

The first group of participants read a label for "Sensi-Shake" and drank a milkshake they believed had 140 calories and 0 grams of fat. Blood tests afterwards showed very little change in their ghrelin levels.

The second group read a label for "Indulgence," a shake they thought had 620 calories and 30 grams of fat. The label convinced participants that they should feel full, and in fact, their ghrelin levels dropped significantly, so they did feel full and satisfied. The only element of the experiment that was different between the two groups was the label on the milkshake.

Discussion:

When food manufacturers market their products, they create labels to appeal to the tastes and interests of consumers. When they target people who want to be healthy, for example, their food labels might include a picture of someone exercising outdoors. Crum's experiment suggests that our ideas about a food product—even before we eat or drink it—may affect us in unexpected ways.

Listening: A Discussion about Food Psychology

Track 2.16   B. Note Taking and   Page 117
C. Note Taking

Abbie: This is really nice. We should go out to dinner together more often.

Patrick: Yes, it's good to see you two, and we've never been here before. This menu looks great; the descriptions of the food sound delicious!

Lydia: I agree, Patrick! This place knows how to appeal to hungry people.

Abbie: You're right, Lydia, the descriptions and photos of the food on the menu would certainly stimulate your appetite if you weren't hungry already. And look, there's a survey card on the table where we can leave comments and rate the food.

Paul: That's a good strategy, actually. If you give customers a chance to give feedback about the food, they feel like they're communicating with the restaurant owners.

Lydia: Right, and communicating with customers is so important nowadays! I mean, look at social media. Businesses are using it to market all kinds of products. It's all about communication. If you can convince people to see your business as a friend or a business partner—you know, instead of just someone who is trying to get their money—it can be a very effective strategy.

Patrick: True, communicating with customers is a real strength of some businesses. And speaking of communication, it's not just connecting on social media that matters to people. Getting together for a meal with friends, family, neighbors—those social connections are another element of food psychology—the role our brain plays.

Paul: Right, like the way those beautiful photos on the menu made us start to feel hungry.

Lydia: Sorry, but I was hungry before we even got here!

Paul: OK, but Patrick makes a very relevant point. The whole food industry—from food manufacturers to grocery stores to restaurants and advertisers—they all know us better than we know ourselves. At least, they understand the psychology of food.

Abbie: That's true, Paul. One way they target us at the grocery store is by displaying a huge variety of foods. We see all of the options in front of us, and what do we do? We find ourselves wanting to buy at least one of everything!

Paul: Abbie knows what I'm talking about. It's the way food looks, the varied options, the social element.

Patrick: Can I ask a question? How does this make you feel? I mean, do you think the food industry has *power* over us and the food we buy? Or the restaurants we decide to go to?

Lydia: Well, understanding food psychology, and understanding the way it might be used to market food—it's really helpful! You can see all the ads, and you can see the beautiful displays at the grocery store, and you can say to yourself, "They're using food psychology to encourage me to buy this." And then you can make a sensible decision and buy what you actually need.

Abbie: Good point, Lydia. Well, you know what they say, knowledge is power.

Paul: Exactly. Well, to get back to what I was saying, our psychology, the way we think, is quite powerful. I heard about one study where they gave people the same milkshake to drink, but half of the people thought it was a low-fat, low-calorie milkshake, and half of the people thought it was super rich and high in calories.

Abbie: I heard about that experiment as well. The people who thought they'd drunk the high-fat, high-calorie drink experienced less hunger afterwards than the other group.

Paul: And they felt full and satisfied because of what their minds told their bodies! The researchers did blood tests, and the two groups actually had different blood chemistry after the experiment! If nothing else, it shows us how much our minds and our attitudes influence our bodies.

Patrick: I see your point, and ahhh I think that's our food.

Lydia: Yep, it is. Great! I hope it tastes as good as it looks!

Speaking

Track 2.17   B.   Page 118

Tips for Marketing your Food Truck

Food trucks have become very popular, but attracting customers isn't always easy. According to Ross Resnick, who created a smartphone app to help customers find food trucks in their cities, "You can't just show up and expect to make a lot of money running a food truck. You have to have a brand and a strategy." Other tips include:

1. If you want to have a successful food truck, work on your photography skills, as well as your cooking skills. Taking beautiful photos of your food for advertising or social media is essential in today's market.
2. Use social media to attract "followers." Then if you send regular updates such as an e-newsletter, customers will remember to stop by for a bite to eat.
3. Learn to cook creatively. International foods in new combinations—from Korean style tacos to fried-chicken sandwiched between breakfast waffles—add to the fun of food-truck dining.
4. Use a creative brand strategy. For example, choose a memorable name and a colorful truck design. This will make you unforgettable to customers.
5. Set up the truck in places where customers can socialize and have fun while they eat. This will encourage them to return and will help you be successful in the food-truck business.

Unit 7: Our Active Earth

LESSON A   Vocabulary

Track 2.18   A. Meaning from Context   Page 124

Inexpensive Buildings for Earthquake Zones

The earth's outer layer consists of several pieces called tectonic plates. The places where these plates meet are called boundaries. Tectonic plates are always moving. Sometimes the plates "jump" as they move. When this happens, earthquakes can occur.

Regions where earthquakes are more likely to occur are called earthquake zones. Some of the countries inside these zones are Pakistan, Haiti, Peru, and Indonesia. All of these countries have experienced major earthquakes, and many people have died because of unsafe buildings. Fortunately, we can construct inexpensive houses that will allow more people to survive earthquakes in developing parts of the world.

Pakistan:

Light walls: Lightweight walls are less affected by earthquakes and are less likely to fall when the ground shakes. In Pakistan, a material called plaster is used to help reinforce the inside and outside of straw walls.

Haiti:

Light roofs: Metal roofs are lighter than concrete and won't collapse when an earthquake occurs.

Small windows: Small windows mean that walls are stronger.

Peru:

Reinforced walls: Walls do not have to be reinforced with steel or other kinds of metal. In Peru, plastic is sometimes used to reinforce walls.

Indonesia:

Enclosed materials: In Indonesia, concrete and metal rods hold brick walls together so that in an earthquake, the whole wall moves as one piece.

Listening: An Earth Science Lecture

Track 2.19   B. Listening for Main Ideas and   Page 126
C. Note Taking   Page 127

OK, so today we're going to continue talking about plate tectonics. As you know, the earth's crust consists of several plates. On this map, the green lines show you the edges of the tectonic plates. These plates are always moving, of course, and *exciting* things happen as a result. The lines you see here on the map, where the tectonic plates come together—those are the earthquake zones. These areas here, in orange and red, are places where earthquakes occur most often. Furthermore, the biggest, most dangerous earthquakes happen in these zones.

Now, when earthquakes occur, there are three different things that might be happening along the boundaries—the places where the earth's plates meet. For your notes, why don't you set up a chart like this one, with four columns and three rows. It will be helpful to you later. In the left-hand column, write "boundary type," "movement," and "results." Notice that I'll be talking about three kinds of boundaries, about how each boundary type is moving, and finally about the result of that movement. OK, as I mentioned, there are three main boundary types. The first kind are called *convergent* boundaries. There, plates come together. This pushing together can cause mountains to form. One plate can also move *under* another at a convergent boundary. That makes the mountains on the top plate rise even higher. In fact, the highest mountains on Earth—the Himalayas, shown here in the photo—are the result of a convergent boundary.

The second type of boundary is called *divergent*. At a divergent boundary, the plates move apart. As they move away from each other, a body of water can form between them. A good example of this is the Arabian Gulf region, where the Arabian Plate and the Eurasian plate moved apart to form the Arabian Gulf and the Gulf of Oman. More recently, the two plates have become convergent again, forming mountains. You can see those at the top of the photo. You don't have to worry about the Arabian Gulf disappearing anytime soon, though, because these changes take place over *millions* of years.

OK, the third and final type of boundary is called a *transform* boundary. There, the plates are moving past each other. To give you an example, along the San Andreas Fault in California and

northern Mexico, one plate is moving north while the other plate is moving south. The plates don't move smoothly, however. The movement actually only happens occasionally, when the plates move in small or large "jumps." And when the plates make a *big* jump, the earth shakes, and we have a major earthquake.

Now, let's take a look at the effects of some recent earthquakes—how they affected people in the world's earthquake zones. In Chile, in 2010, there was a major earthquake. This picture shows an example of buildings that are constructed in the right way for earthquake zones—with strong, reinforced walls, especially if the walls are made of concrete. I know it looks like these buildings were badly damaged in the earthquake, but the buildings actually stayed together in one piece, and that's what you want. Everyone who lived in these buildings probably survived. Another way to build the right kind of buildings for earthquake zones might mean houses with roofs and walls made of lightweight materials that will not collapse—or at least they won't kill you if they do. In this photo from the Philippines in 2017, you can see damage to the road, but these houses—with lightweight walls and roofs—are still standing, and the people who live there are safe. In contrast, living in a part of the world where the buildings *don't* have these features can be quite dangerous. This picture was taken after the 2015 earthquake in Nepal, where many houses collapsed. About 9,000 people died in that earthquake.

So let's look again at our world map. The world's next big earthquake will probably be in one of these areas in yellow, orange, or red. And the number of people who survive the next big earthquake? It depends a lot on the kind of buildings they live in.

Speaking

Track 2.20   A.   Pages 130–131

Living in Japan means knowing a lot about earthquakes. The country experiences an average of 1,500 earthquakes every year! Not all of these are major earthquakes. However, one very large earthquake in the ocean near Japan caused a *tsunami* in the year 2011.

Today, some Japanese people avoid thinking about the horror and sadness of the tsunami of 2011. But a photographer from Argentina went to Japan in 2016 with the goal of helping survivors think about the tsunami in new ways.

Traveling around the world is nothing new to Alejandro Chaskielberg. He has taken pictures and won awards for his photos in several different countries. In Japan, he asked people to consider returning to the places they lived or the places they went before the tsunami. He took new photographs of the people in those places, since many old photographs had been lost or destroyed. According to Chaskielberg, taking these photos "…was a way to help them create new memories."

LESSON B   Vocabulary

Track 2.21   A. Meaning from Context   Page 134

The Pacific Ring of Fire: Fast Facts

1. The Ring of Fire consists of many volcanoes in a near-circle around the Pacific Ocean.
2. Active volcanoes are dangerous. People choose to live near them, however, because volcanic soil is rich and good for farming.
3. In Indonesia, more people live near active volcanoes than in any other country. On the island of Java alone, there are more than 30 volcanoes and about 140 million people.

4. One of the world's worst natural disasters occurred in Indonesia in 1883. The eruption of Mount Krakatau, a volcanic island near Java, caused a tsunami that killed more than 36,000 people. In addition, it produced enough volcanic ash to affect the earth's weather for several months.

5. In Kinarejo, Java, many farmers live near a volcano called Mount Merapi. A man there named Mbah Marijan was known as the "Gatekeeper of Merapi." According to tradition, the Gatekeeper knew the volcano very well, and his job was to tell people when it became dangerous so that they could evacuate. Sadly, Marijan and many others were killed when Mount Merapi erupted violently in 2010.

6. For people who live near volcanoes, evacuating means leaving behind their homes, animals, and daily lives. Therefore, they often wait for definite news about the volcano that will justify their leaving. However, sometimes the news doesn't come in time to save lives.

Listening: A Discussion about Volcanoes

Track 2.22   B. Listening for Main Ideas and   Page 136
C. Listening for Details

Khaled: I'm really glad we're doing this. Studying alone never works well for me.

Ann: I agree. I think studying in a group is really helpful, especially for an exam. So, should we talk about the questions we think might be on the exam?

Khaled: Definitely. I think there will be a question like this: What's the difference between lava and magma? To be honest, I'm not sure I understand the difference. Aren't they the same thing?

Tony: They *are* the same thing—melted rock. But when it's *inside* the earth, it's called magma, and when it comes *out* of the earth, it's called lava.

Ann: According to Chapter 6, that's correct. There's an explanation on page 96. Now, who can give some of the reasons active volcanoes are dangerous? I think there might be a question about that.

Khaled: I'll give it a try. Professor Lopez said that when there's an eruption, hot lava can kill people and start fires. In addition, he talked about huge rocks and hardened lava. I wouldn't want to be nearby when those fly out!

Tony: Me neither! On the other hand, all of that stuff from inside volcanoes makes good soil eventually. And did you guys understand the story about the man in Indonesia—the Gatekeeper? Wasn't his job to tell people when to evacuate or something?

Ann: Yeah, it was, but it's not a very scientific approach.

Tony: Maybe not "scientific," but he had been around the volcano for years. I mean, he probably knew how to read the volcano pretty well.

Ann: That's a good point, but when there *was* a major eruption of Mount Merapi in 2010, the Gatekeeper and a lot of other people died. Personally, I'd rather get my volcano news from scientists. After all, it was geologists working for the U.S. government who told everyone in the area to evacuate before Mount Saint Helens erupted. That was more scientific.

Khaled: And did everyone in the area *listen* to those geologists?

Ann: Actually, when the geologists said the volcano was going to erupt, *almost* everyone left, but some people stayed. They didn't want to leave their homes and everything behind.

Tony: Right. I remember reading about this.

Ann: Mmm. hmmm. Some people stayed, and as a result, 57 people were killed when the volcano erupted. So evacuating at the right time during a natural disaster like that *is* very important.

Tony: Wow! I see what you mean. That kind of danger justifies using the best scientific information, you know, the most definite information you can get instead of listening to a random guy who says he knows the mountain well.

Khaled: I agree, but I think you're missing something about that Gatekeeper guy in Indonesia. He was an important part of village culture, so the people there listened to him.

Ann: Right. That's a good point. Local tradition could affect who people are more likely to listen to—scientists or the Gatekeeper.

Tony: Do you think there'll be a question about the Gatekeeper on the exam?

Track 2.23   D. Listening for Transitions   Page 137

1.

Khaled: Professor Lopez said that when there's an eruption, hot lava can kill people and start fires. In addition, he talked about huge rocks and hardened lava. I wouldn't want to be nearby when those fly out!

Tony: Me neither! On the other hand, all of that stuff from inside volcanoes makes good soil eventually.

2.

Ann: Personally, I'd rather get my volcano news from scientists. After all, it was geologists working for the U.S. government who told everyone in the area to evacuate before Mount Saint Helens erupted. Some people stayed, and as a result, 57 people were killed when the volcano erupted.

Speaking

Track 2.24   Pronunciation: Syllable Number
and Syllable Stress Review   Page 138

col**lapse**	sur**vive**	**dan**gerous	ma**te**rials
e**nough**	**prac**tical	**in**terested	ac**cord**ing	af**fect**

Track 2.25   A.   Page 138

1. common
2. practical
3. circumstances
4. flow
5. summarize
6. clothes
7. psychological
8. recommend
9. reinforce
10. definitely

CD 3

Unit 8: Wonders from the Past

LESSON A   Vocabulary

Track 3.2   A. Meaning from Context   Page 144

An Amazing Discovery

Every career has a high point, and according to National Geographic Explorer William Saturno, being the first human being in 2,000 years to view a beautiful Maya mural in Guatemala was probably that point for him. Saturno, an archaeologist and an expert on the Maya civilization, discovered the mural inside a room that was once next to a pyramid. The mural room and pyramid were later covered by a larger pyramid—part of the ruins of an ancient Maya city, now called San Bartolo.

At first, Saturno could see only a small part of the mural. He had to dig through earth and stone in order to reveal the rest. Then, instead of using a camera, Saturno used his scanner to take digital images of the mural. He took about 350 scans!

The mural wasn't the only important find at San Bartolo. The archaeologists also uncovered a tomb. It was a royal tomb, where the bones of a Maya king were buried, along with objects such as a bowl in the shape of a frog and an image of the Maya rain god Chac.

Listening: A Guided Tour of Uxmal

Track 3.3   B. Listening for Main Ideas and   Page 146
**   C. Listening for Details   Page 147**

Tour Guide: Good morning, and welcome to Uxmal! This ancient city was part of the Maya civilization. It's one of the most fascinating and popular Maya historical sites in Mexico, and for good reason. There's a *lot* to see here! So I hope you all have on comfortable walking shoes today. There are several pyramids and other structures at this site, which were all built by the Maya during the late Classic period. That's around A.D. 600 to 900. So they are not nearly as ancient as the pyramids in Egypt, of course, but they're still pretty old and very special.

There is also a ball court on the site where ball games were played. The ball game the Maya played was a very difficult and dangerous sport, played with a hard ball made of rubber. I'll tell you more about it when we get there. We'll also see tombs where important people were buried—mostly people from one royal family.

I've visited a lot of Maya ruins, and personally, I think the ruins at Uxmal are the most beautiful and interesting of all of them. So, you've picked a good place to visit. Maybe you'll agree with me after our tour today.

OK. Just to let you know, the guided tour takes about 90 minutes, but after that you are welcome to stay and explore the site on your own until closing time. OK, Ready? Great! Let's get started!

Tour guide: The first stop on our tour is this huge pyramid right behind me. It's called the Pyramid of the Magician, and I'm sure you've seen images of this famous pyramid on brochures or in your guide book. Not only is it the *tallest* pyramid at Uxmal, it's also a very unusual pyramid because it has *rounded* sides, and as you know, most pyramids have *flat* sides, like the pyramids in Egypt.

Now, we don't actually know the Maya name for this pyramid, or for any of the structures here at Uxmal. But there is an old story about the pyramid. They say a magician used his powers to build this pyramid in *one night,* and that's why we call it the Pyramid of the Magician. So, how many of you think the story is true? Anyone?

Well, even though we don't know *exactly* how long it took to build the pyramid, we *do* know that it was built in different stages, during different time periods, so it definitely wasn't built in one night. In reality, it took around 300 years to build this structure. And like other Maya pyramids, this one started out small. The workers built a bigger structure on top of the first small pyramid and an even bigger structure on top of that one. Archaeologists have revealed parts of *five* different structures here that make up the pyramid you see today! Does anyone have any questions at this point?

Female tourist: I do have a question. You mentioned archaeologists. When was Uxmal discovered? I mean, in modern times. When was it found?

Tour guide: That's a great question! Of course, in some places, the Maya cities were completely covered over by trees and other plants, and they had to dig to find the buildings underneath. But Uxmal stayed pretty visible over time. People could see the ruins fairly easily. There are drawings from the 1700s and photos from the 1800s, so this has been a popular place to visit for hundreds of years!

OK, I'll give you a minute or two to take photos, and then we'll head over to the ball court and maybe play a ball game. Just kidding.

Male tourist: Could I ask a question?

Tour guide: Absolutely!

Male tourist: Do they still play the Maya ball game here? Like maybe to show the public what the game was like?

Tour guide: No, sorry—not here at Uxmal. OK, after we see the ball court, we'll go to the Governor's Palace. In front of *that* structure is something very special. It's called the *Jaguar Throne.* It's very cool. And as you probably know, a jaguar is a wild cat. It's the largest wild cat in the Americas, and you can still find a few wild jaguars in Mexico today. OK, so the Jaguar Throne in front of the Governor's Palace is made from stone, and it looks like a jaguar with two heads. In the middle is a kind of seat—most likely for a royal person like a king to sit in.

Tour guide Cont'd: Now, here we are at the ball court. OK, so who can tell me about the ball games that were played in this ball court? Anyone?

Speaking

Track 3.4   Pronunciation: Question
**   Intonation   Page 148**

Is the Maya ball game still **played** here?

Would you rather leave now or later?

When was Uxmal **dis<u>co</u>vered**?

Track 3.5   A.   Page 148

1. What time are we leaving?
2. Have you ever been to Kazakhstan?
3. How was the walking tour?
4. Did you go there on Friday or Saturday?
5. Is the mural from the early, middle, or late period?
6. Does this story make sense to you?
7. Is the mural in Mexico, Guatemala, or Honduras?
8. Where's the pyramid?

LESSON B   Vocabulary

Track 3.6   A. Meaning from Context   Page 154

New Clues About Tutankhamen: His Life and Death

In 1922, British Egyptologist Howard Carter found the remains of a young man in a tomb filled with royal treasures in the Valley of the Kings, Egypt. Newspapers around the world reported the discovery and described the gold jewelry, precious stones, and beautiful art found in the tomb. Everyone wanted to know who this important man was.

We now know Tutankhamen was the son of Akhenaten, and he ruled Egypt from 1332–1322 BC. He became pharaoh1 as a child, and he died young. Yet many questions are still unanswered. Was "Tut" ill? Was he murdered2? What did he look like when he was alive?

In 2005, scientists began to analyze Tut's remains with computer tomography (CT) and modern forensic medicine—a science usually used to investigate and solve murder cases. Tut's remains were scanned in a CT machine, which created 3-D images. Using this technology, scientists determined that Tut was probably not murdered and was about 19 when he died.

Scientists also worked with an artist to construct a life-like model of Tut. Not everyone likes the result, but according to the CT scans, he probably looked a lot like modern Egyptians.

Listening: A Conversation about an Assignment

Track 3.7   B. Listening for Main Ideas and   Page 156
C. Note Taking   Page 157

Silvio: Hi, Professor Norton. Thanks for seeing me.

Professor Norton: It's my pleasure, Silvio. How can I help you?

Silvio: Well, I'm having some trouble with the oral summary assignment for Communication 102.

Professor Norton: Right. The oral summary of a movie or documentary film. What are you having trouble with?

Silvio: OK, so, I watched a very interesting documentary about the discovery of a historical site in Vietnam. It's called the Thang Long Imperial Citadel.

Professor Norton: Hmmm. I haven't heard of it.

Silvio: Well, it's in Hanoi, Vietnam. The citadel itself was a place where the royal family—the people who ruled Vietnam at the time—could stay safe. Anyway, they were starting the construction of a new building there, and the workers found some ruins at the site and had to stop.

Professor Norton: Huh. What kind of ruins did they find?

Silvio: Well, for instance, they found the remains of some old buildings that were probably palaces. The pieces were decorative and beautiful, not like parts of regular houses that were built at that time. That's how they determined the buildings were palaces.

Professor Norton: I see. It sounds like an interesting documentary.

Silvio: It was interesting, but the problem is I don't really know how to summarize. Not very well, at least.

Professor Norton: Hmmm. Are these your notes?

Silvio: Yeah. I wrote down a few things while I was watching.

Professor Norton: Actually, they look pretty good. In a way, you've done some summarizing already.

Silvio: I have?

Professor Norton: Sure. You didn't write down every word you heard, right? Everything in your notes looks fairly important, or at least interesting.

Silvio: OK. So what do I do now?

Professor Norton: Well, you could try a technique that newspaper reporters use. Let's call it the "Wh- questions technique for summarizing."

Silvio: Huh. I've never heard of that. How does it work?

Professor Norton: It's pretty easy, really. You ask yourself questions with Who, What, When, Where, Why, and How. To give you an example question, who was involved in the documentary you watched?

Silvio: The Vietnamese government, mostly. They had planned to construct a new government building near the citadel gate.

Professor Norton: Good! And what happened? Or what did they do?

Silvio: They started digging, and they started finding and reporting all these ancient artifacts that were buried there. That's where the archaeologists got involved. The government called archaeologists in to investigate the site and let them know if it was important historically.

Professor Norton: So the people involved were the Vietnamese government and the archaeologists. Then the next question is Why? As in Why were the archaeologists called in? And why were all those old things there at the site?

Silvio: OK. I see what you mean. Who, and what, and why, where, when?

Professor Norton: You got it. The idea is to identify the most important information and to start with that information.

Silvio: That makes sense. But I have a question. What about information that's less important? Like all of the stuff the archaeologists found?

Professor Norton: Actually, a few examples and interesting details can make a summary stronger. I mean, it's one thing to say that they found some old artifacts. But if you can support that idea with one or two examples, it can be a much more effective summary. So, what else did the archaeologists find?

Silvio: Well, for example, they found some dishes and coins there.

Professor Norton: So, things people used in their daily lives.

Silvio: Exactly, and that's why these things were precious to the archaeologists. Since there's no one alive today to tell us what life was like a thousand years ago, we can look at these objects and learn how people lived back then.

Professor Norton: That makes the objects real historical treasures, doesn't it? We can learn a lot by analyzing a plate and finding out how it was made or by finding out whether they preferred plain-looking dishes or colorful, artistic-looking dishes.

Silvio: Exactly! Well, I really appreciate your help, Professor Norton. This Wh- question technique seems really useful. I feel much better about the summary assignment now.

Professor Norton: Well, I'm happy to help, and I'm sure you'll do a great job, Silvio. Oh, and be sure to practice your presentation a few times. That always helps.

Silvio: Thanks, I will. Well, see you Thursday.

Speaking

Track 3.8   A. Note Taking   Page 158

Silvio: Hi everyone, my name is Silvio. And today I'm going to talk about a documentary film I watched. The topic of the film was the discovery of a historical site in Hanoi, Vietnam, called *the Imperial Thang Long Citadel*. OK, this discovery happened in 2002. That's when the Vietnamese government started to construct a new building, but as the construction workers began to dig into the ground, they started to find ruins, such as pieces of old buildings that used to be palaces. Well, the government stopped the construction and called in a team of archaeologists, and it quickly became clear that the Citadel site was very important historically. The archaeologists found many ancient artifacts there—for instance, coins and dishes and other objects from the daily lives of the people who once lived at the site. It's important to note that the Vietnamese government did not move ahead with the construction of a new building at this site. Instead, they worked with archaeologists to investigate the site's historical importance, and they chose a different location for the new building. In 2010, the Citadel became a UNESCO World Heritage Site and is now quite popular with tourists. Now, anyone can visit the Citadel and learn about the people who lived there at different points in history. Thank you for your attention. Are there any questions?

Unit 9: Species Survival

LESSON A   Vocabulary

Track 3.9   A. Meaning from Context   Page 164

The *Beagle* in South America

The *Beagle* expedition's priority was to map the harbors and coastlines of South America. Charles Darwin also spent a lot of his time on land, exploring parts of the Argentine Pampas, the Atacama Desert, and the Andes mountains.

1. **Argentina, 1832:** At both Punta Alta and Monte Hermoso, Darwin found fossils of large prehistoric animals. He could not identify the fossils, but they were similar to modern animal **species** from the area. This might have been the beginning of his now famous idea that species could change over time.
2. **Chile, 1833:** In South America, the men on Darwin's ship the *Beagle* sometimes ate a bird called a *rhea*. Darwin heard about a smaller type of rhea. It lived mostly in southern Patagonia, while the larger rhea lived in the north. Darwin wondered why the southern rhea differed from the northern one. At this time, Darwin became interested in the diversity of animal life. Could an animal's environment affect traits such as size?
3. **Galápagos Islands, Ecuador, 1835:** Here, Darwin began to develop his ideas about why and how the diversity of species occurred. In a process he called natural selection, an animal with a useful trait was more likely to survive, and therefore, more likely to reproduce. The animal's offspring would then inherit the useful trait. In contrast, animals of that same species with a different trait might die and not reproduce. In this way, a species would adapt to its environment and change over time.

Track 3.10   C.   Page 165

Out of Africa

Anthropologists, scientists who study human beings, have long said that modern humans first lived in Africa and then moved east toward Asia, north across the Mediterranean, and later throughout the world.

Now, a large genetic study supports that theory. The study looked at nearly 1,000 people in 51 places around the world. It found the most genetic diversity in Africa and less farther away from Africa. How did this happen? When small groups of people moved away, they took only a small amount of all the possible genetic information with them. People in the small groups reproduced. Their offspring inherited their parents' more limited set of genes. Therefore, their traits were very similar to those of their parents. This process continued as small groups of people moved farther and farther from Africa.

Listening: A Talk about Birds

Track 3.11   B. Listening for Main Ideas and   Page 166
**   C. Listening for Details   Page 167**

Biologist: Welcome, everyone. I'm glad you could come for the presentation today. After my talk, we'll go outside to the gardens, but first I'll show you pictures of some of the birds we're likely to see today. That way you'll be ready to identify these birds when you see them. You are welcome to ask questions, so please don't be shy.

OK. One type of bird I *know* we're going to see today is the finch. In this picture, we see a European goldfinch. These birds are very common here in the UK and in many other parts of Europe—in northern Europe during the summer and farther south during the winter. As you can see, the goldfinch isn't really gold in color, but the trait that makes it easy to identify is this patch of bright yellow feathers on each wing. Now, the goldfinch eats seeds, and one of its favorite seeds comes from inside this flower, the thistle. This flower here. It grows wild, pretty much everywhere, as you know, and not everyone loves it. But it's an important source of food for finches. These birds adapted over time, and the finches we'll see in the gardens today have certain traits, or special features, that help them survive. Their ancestors long ago had these same traits, of course. They helped the birds to live and reproduce, and their offspring inherited these traits—in this case, it's a beak that fits nicely inside the thistle flower. And now we have lots of finches eating lots of thistle seeds!

Female Visitor 1: Excuse me. How can you tell the difference between male and female goldfinches?

Biologist: That's a good question. The males and females of this bird species don't differ much in their appearance. But the one we saw in the last slide is definitely a male. One difference is that the female's beak is a little shorter, so she can't reach as many kinds of flower seeds as the male can. Are there any other questions?

Male Visitor: Yes. Is the goldfinch here all year round?

Biologist: Actually, most of them fly to warmer parts of Europe in September or October. They come back to the UK in the spring. OK. Let's talk about a second type of finch—the greenfinch. The greenfinch has an even wider range than the goldfinch. It lives in most parts of Europe, and also northwest Africa and parts of Turkey.

Female Visitor 1: Is there anything else that's special about the greenfinch?

Biologist: I'm glad you asked! The greenfinch has an interesting trait. Its beak is quite large and strong, and it uses that powerful beak to break open *larger* seeds. Is everything clear so far?

Female Visitor 2: So far, so good—thanks!

Biologist: OK, good, and to summarize: the male goldfinch eats the small seeds inside flowers, the female goldfinch eats other small seeds, and the greenfinch eats larger seeds.

Male Visitor: So, it sounds like there's one kind of bird for each kind of food supply, basically.

Biologist: That's exactly right. Through the process of natural selection, each bird has its own special place in the environment. Think about it this way: if many other birds eat *small* seeds, and you're the only bird that eats *big* seeds, then you'll always have plenty to eat! That kind of diversity means that more species can survive together in the same place. Here you can see just some of the types of birds that visit the gardens each year. Yes? In the back?

Female Visitor 2: I have a question. Does the greenfinch leave the UK in the winter like the goldfinch does?

Biologist: Most of the time, no. They stay here, but you will find them living in different places during different seasons. In the summer, you're more likely to find them in parks and forests. But in the winter, when there is less food, you'll find them in people's gardens and in farmers' fields. Remember, they have those large beaks, so they can eat the seeds and grains that farmers and gardeners leave behind.

Speaking

Track 3.12   A.   Page 168

banana   demand   identify   reproduce

Track 3.13   Pronunciation: Stress in Multi-Syllable Words   Page 168

local   factor   season

analyze

local   factor   season

Track 3.14   B.   Page 168

1. practical 2. compare 3. attachment 4. available 5. proportion 6. support

Track 3.15   C.   Page 168

1. recommend 2. classify 3. atmosphere 4. quantity 5. romantic 6. disappear

Track 3.16   E.   Page 169

The Process of Natural Selection

Here's a brief explanation of the process of natural selection. First, the environment affects animals in some way. Because of this, the animals that have certain helpful traits do well in their environments. And therefore, they survive and reproduce. The offspring of these animals inherit the helpful trait from their parents. Then these offspring grow up, reproduce, and pass the helpful trait onto *their* offspring and so on and so on. This process continues and as a result, over time, most of the animals in the species have the helpful trait.

LESSON B   Vocabulary

Track 3.17   A. Meaning from Context   Page 174

Bar Coding Life on Earth

Paul Hebert is a biologist at the University of Guelph in Canada. As a young man in the 1970s, part of his job was to classify thousands of different species of moths. Finding tiny variations in the moths in order to describe each species scientifically was not easy, however.

In 2003, Hebert suggested something a bit controversial. Instead of using descriptions to identify different species, why not use DNA? Hebert argued that a bar code—similar to the bar codes on products in a store—could be created for every living thing on Earth. This was a major break from scientific tradition.

Hebert suggested using part of a gene called *CO1*, which nearly every form of life has, to create bar codes. This gene is made up of four chemical substances known as *G, T, C,* and *A,* and the sequence of these substances differs for each species. Using bar codes and an electronic catalog, scientists or anyone else can identify a plant or animal by testing a sample of its DNA.

Hebert's bar code technique is not only a good way to identify species, the electronic catalog has also become a public resource that makes people more aware of biodiversity.

Listening: A Conversation about a Photo Project

Track 3.18   B. Listening for Main Ideas and   Page 176 C. Listening for Details   Page 177

Sandra: What an amazing photo. Check it out! It's a red-ruffed lemur!

Robbie: Let's see. Wow! What a beautiful animal! They live in Madagascar, right?

Sandra: Yeah, originally, but this one lives in a zoo.

Robbie: Oh, wait. Is it part of that Photo Ark project? I read something about that recently.

Sandra: Yep. These photos are by Joel Sartore. He's a photographer for National Geographic. He's a nature photographer, and he's concerned about the species that are disappearing, so he wants to take pictures of all of the animal species in human care—that's around 12,000 species—before a lot of them are gone forever. His photos are amazing.

Robbie: Yeah, they are. I remember seeing his photos from around the world—images of animals in their natural habitats. So, why did he start taking pictures of animals that are *not* in their natural habitats?

Sandra: Well, for one thing, there are millions of described species in the wild. He couldn't possibly photograph that many! And in this article, he argues that the photos he's taking now make people care about the animals more than the photos he used to take.

Robbie: Really?

Sandra: Yeah. And he's publishing a lot more photos now. They're showing up on TV and on social media, and people are becoming more aware of endangered species like this lemur.

Robbie: Hmmm. Let me see that photo *again.* I really like the technique he uses—photographing each animal against a plain black or white background. It's very effective. It really gets you to focus on the animal.

Sandra: Yeah, it's pretty cool. I didn't realize there were so many variations within the same species. I wonder how they classify all of them. I mean, look at these bears. This black bear and this brown bear are really different from each other.

Robbie: Yeah, they are pretty different. These are such great photos!

Sandra: They are, but you know, a project like this isn't really enough.

Robbie: What do you mean?

Sandra: Well, these photos might make people aware of endangered species, but if nothing else changes, a lot of these animals will still become extinct one day and be gone forever.

Robbie: Right, and all we'll have left are some photos—and not of every species either. That's just not possible because there are so many of them. In the end, the Photo Ark will really just be a sample of all the species.

Sandra: True. It's so sad to think that so many species will be extinct one day, but I guess photos like Joel Sartore's can help.

Robbie: Right.

Sandra: There's a story in this article about a little brown bird in Florida that was disappearing. It's called the Florida grasshopper sparrow. There were only a few hundred of them left.

Robbie: Wow! That's not very many.

Sandra: It's not, and the wildlife groups there were trying to do something to help. Then one of Sartore's photos—a picture of the bird—was published, and a lot of people saw it. After that, the groups received a *lot* more money from the government to help them in their work.

Robbie: That's *great*!

Sandra: I know. Their funding went from $20,000 to over a *million* dollars!

Robbie: Wow! That's a significant amount of money! So, did they save the sparrow?

Sandra: They're working on it. Several groups are now raising the birds in captivity in order to increase their numbers. I guess if a photo can create a strong reaction in people—and cause a sequence of events like that to happen—then it seems like Joel Sartore's project is making a difference.

Robbie: Good point. So, what about you, Sandra? Are you doing anything to save endangered species?

Sandra: I'm talking with you about them, aren't I? And I'm trying to stay informed about them.

Robbie: I see. So you're not doing anything controversial—like trying to stop the construction of those apartment buildings near the beach?

Sandra: No, Robbie…How about you?

Robbie: As a matter of fact, I donate money every year to an organization that works to protect wildlife. I also try to avoid buying products that contain chemicals or substances that are harmful to the environment.

Sandra: Good for you! That's great! I didn't know that about you.

Robbie: Well, my grandfather was really interested in wildlife. He used to go on nature walks almost every weekend, so I guess it's in my genes or something.

Speaking

Track 3.19   A.   Page 178

Matt: Jessica? It's me!

Jessica: Matt! It's great to hear your voice! Are you back home now?

Matt: Yes, and I really missed you, but I'm so happy you talked me into going on the expedition! I can't believe I almost turned down such a great opportunity.

Jessica: Tell me all about it!

Matt: Well, we were high up in the Foja Mountains. No human beings have ever lived there!

Jessica: How exciting! Did you get a lot of work done?

Matt: We did! We set up a tent as our laboratory. It was small but fine.

Jessica: Did it rain a lot?

Matt: Every day. Well, one afternoon the sky cleared up for a while, but the clouds were back by that evening. It was OK, though. The frogs didn't mind the rain.

Jessica: Oh, tell me about the frogs!

Matt: Can you believe there are 350 frog species in New Guinea? The best time to find them is at night. When I turned on my flashlight, I could see them easily and pick them up with my hands.

Jessica: How interesting! It sounds like it was a great trip.

Matt: It was, and the lead scientist was really happy with my work.

Jessica: That's great! Congratulations, Matt!

Unit 10: Entrepreneurs and Innovators

LESSON A   Vocabulary

Track 3.20   A. Meaning from Context   Page 184

Six Traits of Successful Entrepreneurs

What does it take to be a successful entrepreneur? Here are six common traits.

1. **Caring about More than Money:** Making money is usually not the main motivation for successful entrepreneurs. Instead, they are driven by a strong belief in their product or service and its potential to improve people's lives in some way.
2. **Not Giving Up:** Good entrepreneurs are persistent. They don't give up easily and are willing to try out new ideas and take risks. Doing this leads to some failures along the way, but the entrepreneurs who eventually succeed are the ones who do not quit when things go badly.
3. **Having a Vision:** True entrepreneurs see opportunities where most people do not. Then they need to convince investors to lend money for new kinds of products and services.
4. **Dealing with Change:** Being open-minded and flexible is another important trait for entrepreneurs. The product they imagined in the beginning is likely to evolve over time, so they need to continue to be flexible.
5. **Tolerating Uncertainty:** Entrepreneurs must be able to live with uncertainty. Nobody can predict the future, but good entrepreneurs keep moving ahead with their ideas rather than worrying about the unknown.
6. **Having Self-Confidence:** The sixth essential trait of successful entrepreneurs is psychological—having confidence in oneself. The best entrepreneurs believe in themselves and their ideas.

Listening: A Presentation about a Success Story

Track 3.21   B. Listening for Main Ideas and   Page 186
C. Listening for Details   Page 187

Hello. Good morning, and thank you for inviting me to speak at the fourth annual Innovations in Business conference. It's a pleasure to be here. My topic this morning is something that is—I can see—very relevant to many of you. Many of you have paper cups in your hands right now. It's *coffee*—and a little company called Starbucks that all of you have heard of. And although the company isn't actually "little" anymore, it did start out that way. I'd like to talk to you today about the man who started the company—Howard Schultz—and about some of the things he's done along the way that have led to the company's great success. Perhaps these same ideas could lead to more success for your companies as well.

In the early days, Schultz was like every entrepreneur. He had a strong motivation—to bring the coffee culture of European countries to the United States—but of course, he needed money to get started, so he needed to find investors. But it was quite difficult for Schultz to find those investors for two main reasons— First, they didn't understand why anyone would pay extra for a fancy cup of coffee, and this created a lot of uncertainty about the whole idea. Would they eventually get their money back? *Now*, of course, it seems like the world was just waiting for a good café latte to come along. I've certainly bought my share of fancy coffee drinks. OK, the other reason for the uncertainty among possible investors was the fact that Schultz kept talking about using his company to *do good things*. That was unusual, since the main focus of most businesses is making money. If you ask me, focusing only on making money is a great way to make a business *fail*, but I suppose a lot of people would disagree with me on that.

So what is Starbucks' model for success? To begin with, valuing employees is an essential part of the Starbucks business model, and it's an idea that many businesses could learn from, I think. In fact, I really shouldn't use the term *employees* to refer to the people who work at Starbucks, since they're actually called *partners*. As you know, partners in a company are equals, so I guess Starbucks wants to show its employees how important they are to the company. A well-known quotation from Schultz is that, "Success is best when it's shared." and Starbucks does share its profits with its employees—sorry—with its *partners*! Not only are Starbucks wages a little higher than in other service jobs, partners who work enough hours can receive stock in the company. I mean, how great is that?! If Starbucks has a good year, their employee stockholders also have a good year. Now, let's think back to a younger Howard Schultz trying to convince investors that instead of keeping employees' salaries as low as possible— you know, in order to make a bigger profit—he was planning to pay his employees more in order to make their lives better. It must have been a difficult idea for the investors to accept. Well, Schultz was persistent, and he had confidence in his ideas—And in light of how quickly Starbucks grew, that persistence clearly paid off. Another important aspect of the Starbucks business model has been to treat the customers as individuals and to value them as people. It's no accident that your name is hand-written on your coffee cup and that the coffee can be customized in any number of ways to suit your taste. According to the company website, "Our mission is to inspire and nurture the human spirit – one person, one cup, and one neighborhood at a time."

OK. As long as we're trying to learn lessons from Schultz and his company, it's important to point out that Starbucks has experienced some failures along the way. Schultz has given up his position as CEO on more than one occasion over the years. The first time was in 2000, and the company experienced some major problems as a result. Those problems were caused by the company moving away from Schultz's original vision. Instead, after Schultz quit, they moved away from being a company that cared about its employees and focused on making as much money as possible. And though every company evolves over time, this was not the kind of change that Schultz wanted. Starbucks' sales were down, and some stores had been closed when Schultz returned to the company in 2008. So in the hope of turning the company around, he outlined a set of plans for social responsibility—buying coffee only from ethical growers, doing community service, and

making Starbucks stores more environmentally sustainable. And although he quit the job of CEO again more recently, he stayed on with the company in a new position, his goal now being the same as it was in the beginning—to have a successful company that also does good things. And this is where we can find a valuable lesson to take away from the Starbucks story. Customers have supported this company for many years now and made it a success, and that's at least partly because customers are willing to spend a little more to buy products from a business that has strong values and that acts responsibly. They want to feel good about the companies they buy from, and any company that wants to be successful needs to keep this in mind. Thanks, and we do have a few minutes for questions.

Speaking

Track 3.22   Pronunciation: Thought Groups   Page 189

In the early days, / Shultz was like / every entrepreneur.

The company experienced / some major problems / as a result.

Track 3.23   C.   Page 189

1. My best friend started her own company/ about five years ago/ right after college.
2. Her son wants to study business/ and then work at a bank.
3. Running a successful business is not easy / because you work a lot / and have to take risks.
4. I got a job/ at the new café/ on Main Street.
5. If you work hard/ and treat people well/ you'll be successful.
6. After work / I usually take a walk / so I can relax / and get some exercise.

LESSON B   Vocabulary

Track 3.24   A.   Page 194

Chanda Shroff

When Chanda Shroff visited a part of India known as Kutch, she saw the potential for village women there to earn an income by selling their beautiful embroidery work. Shroff thought there was a strong probability that other people would appreciate the beautiful embroidery as much as she did, so she commissioned 30 embroidered *saris* before she left Kutch. Evidently, she was right. The saris caused considerable excitement at an art exhibit in Mumbai. Shroff sold all 30 of them within a few hours.

Shroff eventually founded an innovative organization called *Shrujan*. Its mission is to market this traditional craft and help the Kutch people become more self-sufficient and to keep the craft alive and evolving. Since the Shrujan organization was founded, it has helped over 22,000 women earn sustainable, home-based income for their work and achieve more financial security. Shrujan has received a lot of recognition for its work, and Shroff herself received a Rolex Award for Enterprise in 2006. Shroff died in 2016, but the Kutch people still love and respect this woman who made a significant difference in so many people's lives.

Listening: A Conversation about Jack Andraka

Track 3.25   B. Listening for Main Ideas and   Page 197
C. Listening for Details

Olivia: This is nice, Brooke. We hardly ever have time to meet for coffee anymore.

Brooke: I know, and we always have a lot to talk about.

Olivia: We do! How is your family doing?

Brooke: Oh, most of us are fine. Thanks for asking, Olivia.

Olivia: What do you mean *most* of you?

Brooke: Yeah, well, we got some bad news about one of my cousins. He has cancer—lymphoma, I think it is. Fortunately, they found it pretty early, and he's getting treatment.

Olivia: Well, that's good, but I'm really sorry to hear that.

Brooke: Thanks. I appreciate it. How about you and your family?

Olivia: Everybody's fine. My brother Mike changed jobs and is now working at a start-up company that one of his college friends founded a couple of years ago. Other than that, no big family news. I'm really busy at work these days, but I did have enough time on my lunch break yesterday to read a really interesting article.

Brooke: Oh, yeah? What was it about?

Olivia: Coincidentally, it was kind of about cancer. Well, it was really about a young man who developed an innovative test for cancer. And he's one of those people who makes you feel like you haven't achieved much in life!

Brooke: Why do you say that?

Olivia: Well, he's so *young*! And he was only in *high school* when he started to work on this test. It's a test for a few different types of cancer.

Brooke: What's his name?

Olivia: Jack Andraka. He had a really good family friend who died of pancreatic cancer, and ever since then, it's been Andraka's mission to find a better, cheaper medical test for it.

Brooke: Wait, I've heard of this guy! I saw a video of a presentation he gave. You know, it's the same with any type of cancer. Evidently, if doctors can detect it early, there's a higher probability that you can be treated and *survive*.

Olivia: Right. Well, Jack has gotten a lot of recognition—all kinds of attention and awards for developing the test. The test he developed is cheap. It's just a special piece of paper that costs around 3 cents, and it only takes 5 minutes.

Brooke: That sounds great.

Olivia: Yeah, especially compared with the existing test. That one is really expensive, and not very accurate. The worst thing about that test, though, is that it doesn't detect the cancer early enough.

Brooke: And that's so important. So, when will the new test be available?

Olivia: As soon as they can make it available, I guess, but it will definitely take some time. Anything new like this—especially anything new in medicine—takes a considerable amount of testing. They have to make sure it works and everything.

Brooke: That's true. It sounds like the test has a lot of potential to save lives, at least eventually.

Olivia: Yeah, it does. And can you believe he got the idea when he was just a *teenager*?

Brooke: That's amazing.

Olivia: I know, right? I also get the feeling he's not going to try to get rich from the invention. I don't know for sure, but I think he wants the test to remain inexpensive. That way everyone will be able to afford it, no matter what their income level is. He's a remarkable young man!

Brooke: I know. It's impressive. It sounds like his new test will really help people and save lives. He was funny, too, when I saw that video of him giving his talk.

Olivia: I'll look online for that. I'd be interested in watching it and hearing him speak. I can also send you the link to that article if you want.

Brooke: Sure. That would be great. Thanks.

VIDEO SCRIPTS

Unit 1: Bee Therapy

Narrator: Today in parts of Asia, people from all walks of life are choosing to be stung by bees—often dozens of times in one sitting. Hso-rong Chen is battling multiple sclerosis, a disease which slowly causes the body's nerves to deteriorate.

Hso-rong Chen, Patient: For six months I was bedridden. I could not move. I would have symptoms of tingling and numbness in my hands. It was excruciating pain.

Narrator: Then Hso-rong heard about bee-sting therapy. For help, she turned to Mr. Cheng-yi Chen, Bee-Sting Therapy Master—a trained master who has practiced bee-sting therapy for 12 years. Every week, Mr. Chen and his assistants treat 200 patients and sacrifice 6,000 honeybees. The results, he says, can be astounding.

Mr. Cheng-yi Chen, Bee-Sting Therapy Master: After 600 bees, you will look 5 years younger than your contemporaries.

Narrator: But can bee stings really help Hso-rong fight multiple sclerosis? She began an intensive course of therapy, receiving over 200 stings a week for months on end. Honeybees only sting once, and they die soon after. But even separated from the bee, the stinger continues to inject venom into its victim. The body responds with a flood of histamines and white blood cells. And soon the area becomes hot, red, swollen, and itchy.

Hso-rong Chen: He gives me one sting. I don't even have time to feel the pain before he stings me again. And the pain lasts for 1 hour.

Narrator: Many think it is based on the 5,000-year-old practice of acupuncture—a proven treatment for pain. Although today

Mr. Chen sees bee acupuncture as a labor of love, even he once considered it taboo. In fact, like most of us, he was afraid of bees. Thirty years ago, Mr. Chen was an executive for a textiles company. Then his wife began to suffer from arthritic pains so severe she couldn't cook or even stand up straight. Western medicines didn't do much good. But when she told her husband she wanted to get stung by bees, he thought the idea was ridiculous.

Mr. Cheng-yi Chen: Naturally, as an educated man, I was against it. We just did not understand bees.

Narrator: But Mr. Chen completely changed his mind when he saw his wife's sudden improvement.

Mr. Cheng-yi Chen: After 3 months, her red blood cell count increased. Her headache disappeared. I was so surprised, I decided to dive into this mysterious treatment and collect all the information that I could.

Narrator: Mr. Chen vowed to devote his life to bringing bee-sting therapy to others. After 6 months of bee-sting therapy, Hso-rong Chen has seen a dramatic change. She insists the therapy has relieved her multiple sclerosis and given her a new lease on life. While most Western-trained doctors would likely say her illness is in remission, Hso-rong is convinced the stings have helped her walk again. It will take years of study before we'll know whether bee stings can relieve arthritis or multiple sclerosis or even the common cold. But whether Hso-rong's recovery is in her head or her hands and feet, for the first time in more than a year, she feels she can resume living. A therapy most of us would find taboo is allowing her to face the future with renewed hope.

Unit 2: Can Robots Learn to Be More Human?

Man 1: I think everybody looks at the robot and ascribes their own human features to it because it does have two sets of cameras that sort of look like eyes. It is sort of designed to give you a sense of being a person and working in human spaces.

What we're really trying to do is get robots out of the lab and into use with people. And figure out, you know, how are robots going to be able to help people do more, accomplish more things and also improve the quality of life of everybody across society.

There are certain examples that we think are really compelling:. being able to assist the disabled, being able to help the elderly. But the real barriers to entry right now are accessibility. Robots still cost a lot; they're still difficult to interface with.

Traditionally, I've worked in the areas of robot learning from demonstration where you don't have to be a programmer to control the robot—to program the robot. There's many different ways you can actually teach a robot.

One is you can just show the robot what you want it to do; you can have the robot watch you do something. But that's really hard because the robot now has to track your movements and has to perceive what are the things that you're interacting with.

A much easier approach is to just take the robot's arm and guide the robot's arm through the motions that you want it to execute.

Another approach is to treat the robot as a remote control device. You take the robot's perspective, and you're joy sticking the robot through the actions you want it to execute.

Once we do those demonstrations, our task is to take that data, apply machine learning and statistical techniques to it such that we can extract, essentially, a mapping from what the robot sees at a given time to what action we want it to take.

We'd love to make it based on what we call "natural language commands" so that you can tell the robot, you know, "Can you pick up that glass for me?" And it would. It would pick up the glass for you.

Man 2: I just want to show the suitable technologies—beam remote presence device.

So I can access this system from anywhere around the world. So I was sitting right here where Aaron's sitting this morning. I was like, "All right, I just want to go check in on the lab." So I've beamed into the system and essentially drove around my lab. I can just do this myself.

In addition to not being reliant upon somebody to just be there to take the call, I can also affect physical change in the world— literally change the world.

Man 1: Robotics is really an extension of the Information Technology Revolution that we've had over the past few decades.

What computing did over the last 40 years are the same things that robotics will provide now. Except that we have more wisdom about the technology to do it better, to make it, you know, to not just think about how these systems are going to improve our productivity and help us do more. But also think about how we can improve everybody's life across the world, across the socioeconomic spectrum.

Unit 3: Faces of India

Steve McCurry: My name is Steve McCurry. I'm a photographer. I started my photography career in college. When I got out of school, the first job that came along was working on a newspaper. But my real ambition was to find a profession in photography which would allow me to travel and see the world. I've been working almost continually with National Geographic for 30 years.

There's no place in the world that has the depth of culture like India.

Narrator: For National Geographic photographer Steve McCurry, India is one of his favorite subjects. Full of color and culture, including some remote villages, Rajasthan is a large Indian state north of Mumbai on the Pakistan border, home to some nomadic shepherds.

Steve McCurry: It's really like going to another planet. The landscape, the way people dress, their traditions, the religion, the music, the food. Almost everything about is kind of strange and also very wonderful. The people are very gentle and hospitable, so I feel very comfortable in Rajasthan. I feel at home.

Narrator: Once the big excitement of Steve's visit calms down a bit, he is able to walk through the streets and meet the villagers.

Steve McCurry: The people here are very interesting and very visual. Some of the nomads are entertainers, snake charmers; they tell stories; they're fortune tellers. But now they're having to find new ways to make a living. I think I'm naturally a shy person, and my first choice is not really to go up and kind of confront people and talk to people and ask people if I can take their picture. But it's something that I have to do, and once I kind of get warmed up, once kind of the wheels start to move, then it becomes very natural, and I'm very happy and very interested in meeting people and talking to villagers.

Steve McCurry (talking about one villager): Okay. 1, 2, 3. Great. Perfect. Tell him I want him to come to New York. I could be his agent. He tells fortunes; he does magic tricks; he is a snake charmer. I think we could [work together]. I think it's the whole face that tells a story. It's not just the eyes or the other features, I think it's the totality of the particular look. Somehow it all kind of works together to tell a story. It's not one particular feature: it's all of them working together. That's it. Perfect.

Unit 4: Dam-Release Rafting

Jonny Phillips: Dams don't always hold water back. Sometimes they have to let it through. For example, if there's a threat to the dam's integrity, or they need to increase supply downriver, then they'll open the valves.

Richard Ambrose: Go on Jonny, really let it rip!

Jonny Phillips: Right.

Richard Ambrose: Go on! [Laughs] Look at that! Jonny, you've broken it!

Narrator: This valve alone can release over 8,000 liters of water a minute.

Richard Ambrose: Now that is a lot of water! Turn it off! Turn it off!

Richard Ambrose: Now there are a few dams in the country where a release of water can be requested by anyone.

Jonny Phillips: You might be a farmer downriver who just needs a bit more water released to irrigate their land.

Richard Ambrose: Or an environmental group concerned that lower water levels downriver are compounding the effects of pollution.

Jonny Phillips: But you do have to pay. For water to be released for a whole day, it can cost 1,500 pounds.

Narrator: But despite the cost, an increasing number of people are requesting the release of water so they can enjoy thrill-seeking recreational pursuits!

Jonny Phillips: And one of the most popular of those leisure activities on this river is whitewater rafting. But just how much difference can a release of water from a dam upriver make?

Richard Ambrose: Well, we're not moving at all at the moment, and the river is just flowing gently, but we've been told that they're going release a load of water from the dam up above, and this river is going to turn into a monster.

Narrator: With the dam open, the amount of water flowing down this river increases to a massive 900 million liters. That's 50 times the normal amount, which means the boys will be travelling down it 10 times faster than normal!

Jonny Phillips: This is the biggest drop of the river.

Richard Ambrose: That's a big one! Oh, my word!

Jonny Phillips: Oh, my word!

Richard Ambrose: Here's the big 'un!

Richard Ambrose: Without that dam up there, we couldn't do this today. And more and more places across the UK are taking advantage of dams to have fun! Let's do it again! Come on!

Jonny Phillips: Sounds like a damn good idea to me!

Richard Ambrose: For that, you're carrying the raft, mate.

Unit 5: 3-D Brain Scans

Man 1: I'm trying to introduce the study of the brain to a bunch of students. I said "If understanding everything you needed to know about the brain is a mile," I asked the students, "how far have we walked in this mile?"

I got answers. Three-quarters of a mile, half a mile. Someone said a quarter mile. And I said, "I think about 3 inches."

This is unconventional science. There's just this huge gap in our knowledge about how brains work, partially because we have no idea what they actually are made up of at the finest level.

When it comes to the nervous system, there are a large number of diseases where the only real sign that there's something wrong is the outward manifestation of the disease.

A person is acting crazy or they don't seem to learn very well, or their movements are disordered in some way.

But if you look at their brain, most of the techniques we have, there's nothing to see.

You've got to see the wires. You just have to see them. And you have to see where they come from, where they go, what they connect with and be able to map that out in enough detail that ultimately you will be able to render the information that goes into a brain to see the wiring diagram at the resolution of every single synaptic vesicle in every synapse. Enough resolution so that we can see everything in a wiring diagram.

I'm a lab head of a group of people who work together. It's kind of a shifting group of people. But it's difficult work, and it requires many kinds of experts. So there are lots of people working together on this project.

Man 2: What we're trying to understand is how cells in the brain communicate with each other.

I have to look at the entire pipeline from the beginning where we start with a mouth. Make a sample. Process the tissue. Cut sections. And then ultimately begin imaging them.

The slice is like you're cutting in a loaf of bread except you're trying to slice very thin pieces of tissue.

So for a millimeter depth, you get about 33,000 sections.

Man 1: Each section of the brain is next to the section that was sliced just before it, and the slice right after it is the next frame.

And if you play these frames in sequence, you see the brain not over time, but over space as if you're looking deeper and deeper into the brain.

The big objects you see that appear and then slowly go out of appearance. Those are nerve cells that are being cut through. And coming off of these cells are these large, light-colored objects, which are the dendrites.

Every little object in here is a little wire to keep track of these cells from one section to another. What you'd like to do is kind of color them in. So every one of these colors have no meaning other than to keep track of each object from section to section.

What this allows us to do is to generate a wiring diagram based on this.

We now know everything about these wires here, and from that, we can generate all the connections of every cell in that area.

Information forces you into this uncomfortable position, where you have to kind of say, "Okay. I don't get it, but I know that the real world is more complicated than the way I'm thinking about it." I feel it's a very long road and we've just started. That's my view.

Unit 6: The Food and Culture of Oaxaca

Narrator: Let's travel to Mexico now, to the historic state of Oaxaca. It's a place that's famous for its traditions—and its food. If you feel cold in winter, you can warm up in Oaxaca by enjoying its spicy chilies, its beautiful dances, and its lovely streets and buildings. When you come to Oaxaca, beautiful colors and wonderful smells are all around you. Oaxaca is one of the poorest states in Mexico, but it's rich in culture. And Oaxacan food is famous around the world.

Susana Trilling, Cooking Instructor: It's one of the best foods. It's very complex.

Narrator: Susana Trilling loves the chiles in Oaxacan food. She moved here 14 years ago to start her own cooking school. Many foreigners have come to learn how to make real Oaxacan *mole* and other dishes. Susana's students heard about Oaxacan food in their own countries. And they come here wanting to learn more. People stay in Oaxaca and take cooking classes at the school. Oaxacan food developed a long time before people came from Europe to America. Tradition is keeping this food alive, and Susana thinks Oaxacan food is as interesting and difficult to make as Thai food or French food. It uses many different ingredients. The first step in cooking Oaxacan food is making a sauce called *mole*. Mole is made from chile peppers, spices, and various other ingredients. Mole is standard in many different Oaxacan dishes. People serve it with chicken and meat, and everything else. But Oaxacan culture is more than just food. The state is also famous for its dances. This dance is centuries old. It's called the *Guelagetza*. It tells about the culture, history, and music of the Oaxacan people. The buildings in the city are large and beautiful. Many of them are Mexican national treasures. This building is 500 years old, with fountains, gardens, and archways. In the past, it was a government building. Today, it's a luxury hotel. Oaxacan people say that a healthy person is happy and loves to work and eat. After a short visit to Oaxaca, you can see that that tradition is still true.

Unit 7: Volcano Trek

Narrator: Millions of years ago, man's earliest ancestors lived in a far region of Ethiopia. In this area, hot lava has erupted from the Erta Ale volcano for about 100 years. The temperature of this lava is more than 2,000 degrees Fahrenheit. Now, a team of explorers is going to see Erta Ale for themselves. They want to learn more about the volcano. It's not an easy trek, and the team has to use camels. They finally reach the crater. Franck Tessier and Irene Margaritis are geologists and professors at the University of Nice. They've traveled halfway around the world to see Erta Ale. Deep in the crater, they see the black lava lake.

Professor Irene Margaritis: It is quite exciting. I want to see it now.

Narrator: Erta Ale is in the Afar area of Ethiopia. The Afar triangle is in an area where three continental plates meet. These plates move farther apart every year. The Erta Ale volcano has the oldest lava lake in the world. The lake is also one of the lowest points on Earth. At Erta Ale, geologists study how the world started millions of years ago. Red hot lava comes out from deep in the earth. This lava forms Erta Ale's lava lake. As the lava cools down, it becomes hard and black. Hot magma breaks through this covering as the volcano erupts. The geologists stand at the top of the active volcano and wait at the side of the crater. It's not easy to be there; there is a strong smell of sulfur. Even in the early morning, it's very, very hot. Then the group goes down into the crater. Professor Tessier wants to collect samples of the red-hot lava. It's 2 o'clock in the morning before they return. They're very tired and, as Professor Margaritis says

Irene Margaritis: Very hot!

Professor Franck Tessier: I think this is fresh lava.

Narrator: The pieces didn't come directly from the lava lake. However, the team decides they're fresh enough. The team will now go back to analyze the samples. As professors, they want to learn new information that they can teach to others. However as geologists, they want to know what the lava of Erta Ale may teach them about how the world began millions of years ago.

Unit 8: Sarah Parcak: Space Archaeologist and Egyptologist

Sarah Parcak: For me, the most important thing about being an explorer is being outside. You know, I grew up camping. I grew up hiking. I grew up with a real appreciation for being outside and really a respect and a wonder for the world around me.

So it's just so critical that we get off our computers and our iPads and our iPhones, and we get up and we look at the world around us. Because ultimately, anytime you're exploring—whether you're beneath the ocean, whether you're on top of a mountain, whether you're excavating a pyramid—you're outside. And it's that curiosity about what makes the world tick that really drives us to explore further.

I'm a space archaeologist. That doesn't mean that I'm using satellites to look into outer space. It's the other way around. I'm using satellites to map and model ancient civilizations. I use a combination of NASA, spy, and high- resolution satellite images literally to look beneath the ground, to find missing cities, pyramids, and lost tombs.

I use information that works almost exactly like a space-based x-ray that allows me to peel away layers of sand, soil, and vegetation to see what lies beneath.

I've been doing this work for the past 10 years in Egypt, and I've been able to find over 3,000 previously unknown ancient settlements. But the best part is I then get to go on and explore them.

You know, for me, I don't think there was ever a single moment that I've had in my life that I could point to me waking up one day and thinking "Aha, that's it. I'm going to be an archaeologist. I'm going to be an explorer."

I think, you know, this started from when I was a very young child, you know. And I read voraciously and read *National Geographic*. I eventually, you know, every now and then a documentary would come on about Egypt. As I got older, I'd go to museums. So this was a love and a passion that was—that grew and was nurtured over time.

And, you know, I will never forget the day that I first landed in Egypt, and the plane actually landed in the middle of the morning. And the pilot actually took a slight detour and flew over the pyramids, so seeing them for the first time with my own eyes was just magical.

I guess the pyramids, to me, are a great symbol of why I love Egypt. And I love ancient cultures because it shows us that the human spirit can endure. And that's really inspiring.

I think, you know, for me, you know my philosophy of dealing with archaeology is it's not about finding stuff. It's not about finding shiny things. What is gold and shiny in archaeology is not the jewelry that you might think. It's the questions that we can ask to help us to understand the past. You know, how did past peoples interact with their environments? What did they do when their economies had problems like we do today?

What about when there was a crisis—an environmental crisis? Archaeology is critical to helping us understand who we are and why we're here. And if we don't protect it, if we don't preserve it, we're going to lose this massive amount of knowledge about how we got to this place. And of course, even more importantly, how we can move ahead. By understanding the past, by asking these big questions, we're able to understand our own world that much better.

My name is Sarah Parcak. I'm a space archaeologist. And I'm a National Geographic Explorer.

Unit 9: Amazing Chameleons

Narrator: With their independently rotating eyes, color-change abilities, their pincer-like feet, their long tongue that they project out of their mouth, and their slow deliberate movements, chameleons are animals that most people would regard as highly charismatic.

One of the centers of chameleon diversity is Madagascar. And of the 202 chameleon species that are currently described to science, 42% occur on Madagascar.

One of the old theories as to why chameleons change color was that they were changing color to match their background. But what we now know is that it's actually a communication strategy. Male-male combat will elicit some of the most impressive colorations from males.

From females, on the other hand, if a female is gravid or she has eggs and is not interested in breeding, if a male starts to try and court her, she will display some very intense, vibrant colorations to let the male know that she's not interested.

In 2015 scientists have discovered that the superficial layer of chameleon skin has pigments in it. And under that there are cells with small guanine crystals. Chameleons change color by actively tuning the spacing between these guanine crystals. And what that does is it changes the wavelength of light that is reflected off of those crystals and thereby changes the hue or the color of the chameleons.

Now chameleons have always been considered a master of camouflage, and some of that is actually behavioral. When chameleons are moving in the branches or moving along the ground, they do a very characteristic back-and-forth motion. And what they're actually doing is mimicking a leaf or a branch in the wind and trying to break up a typical movement pattern of an animal running from a predator.

The chameleon tongue is actually a highly complex array of bone, elastic elements, and muscle. Chameleons can project their tongues up to two body lengths from their mouth. Now this is done at speeds of about 5.8 meters per second, or about 13 miles an hour.

Thirty-six percent of chameleon species are threatened with extinction. There are nine species which are regarded as critically endangered and 37 species that are regarded as endangered.

The main threats to chameleons in the wild is actually habitat alteration and deforestation. Because some chameleons are found only in a specific type of habitat on a single mountain, this makes them highly range restricted. But when that range restriction is combined with other pressures on their habitat, a lot of these species become endangered.

Chameleons have fascinated scientists and naturalists for centuries. And it's something that we're still learning a lot about.

Unit 10: Eco-Fuel Africa

Sanga Moses: My name is Sanga Moses, and I am a National Geographic Explorer.

In 2009, on my way home from Kampala, I met my younger sister carrying wood. When she saw me, she started crying. She had to miss school again in order to gather wood for my family.

Kids in Uganda spend a lot of time carrying wood because their families need it for cooking. A lot of them can't go to school because they don't have the time. This inspired me to think about an alternative source of fuel. I thought about what I could do and decided to quit my job. Everyone was shocked.

I asked a university professor for some advice on what I should do about my idea. I managed to get some help from his students. After 2 months, I had no more savings left. I decided to sell my furniture and even my bed. Slowly, we found a way to create clean cooking fuel using farm waste like corn waste. This fuel burns cleaner and longer and is 65 percent cheaper. Now, I am the CEO of Eco-Fuel Africa.

We work with many farmers and women. They help to sell our Eco-Fuel to their communities. About 105,000 families are already using this fuel on a daily basis in Uganda. And in the next 10 years, we want to reach 16 million families.

By bringing clean cooking fuel to people, we are saving forests, stopping air pollution, and helping farmers and women earn money for their families. More kids can now use the time for gathering wood to study in school instead.

My advice to teens would be to follow your heart. It is amazing what can happen if you believe in your dreams and act upon them.